CYCLE TOURING IN WALES

About the Author

After years of road running and mountaineering wreaked havoc with his knees, Richard Barrett returned to long-distance cycling in his fifties when he bought himself a classic British-made touring bike. Now in his sixties, he rides a handmade bike from one of the great British frame makers that have appeared in recent years. Combined with walking, cycling allows him to continue his love affair with the more mountainous parts of the UK, which he first visited as a teenager.

Richard spent his career in marketing in a number of multinational organizations in the UK and abroad, but he now lives in West Cheshire and rides two or three times a week with groups on both sides of the border.

Other Cicerone guides by the author
Cycling in the Hebrides
Cycling in the Lake District
Cycling Lôn Las Cymru
The Hebridean Way
Walking on Harris and Lewis

CYCLE TOURING IN WALES

A TWO-WEEK CIRCUIT AND SHORTER TOURS
by Richard Barrett

JUNIPER HOUSE, MURLEY MOSS,
OXENHOLME ROAD, KENDAL, CUMBRIA LA9 7RL
www.cicerone.co.uk

Printed in China on behalf of Latitude Press Ltd
A catalogue record for this book is available from the British Library.
All photographs are by the author unless otherwise stated.

Route mapping by Lovell Johns www.lovelljohns.com
© Crown copyright 2019 OS PU100012932.
NASA relief data courtesy of ESRI

Dedication

This book is dedicated to Mr Edward Wood and his orthopaedic team at the Countess of Chester Hospital, who had me back in the saddle a mere 12 weeks after fitting me with a dynamic hip screw to repair a fractured hip that resulted from foolishly venturing out when there was still black ice about. Don't worry, I won't be doing it again.

Acknowledgements

My thanks to Jonathan and Joe Williams of Cicerone for commissioning this book and introducing me to wonderful parts of the country I had never previously visited. I should also like to thank my copyeditor Victoria O'Dowd, Sian, Verity and the production team, who once again made the process such a pleasure.

Updates to this Guide

While every effort is made by our authors to ensure the accuracy of guidebooks as they go to print, changes can occur during the lifetime of an edition. Any updates that we know of for this guide will be on the Cicerone website (www.cicerone.co.uk/988/updates), so please check before planning your trip. We also advise that you check information about such things as transport, accommodation and shops, locally. Even rights of way can be altered over time. We are always grateful for information about any discrepancies between a guidebook and the facts on the ground, sent by email to updates@cicerone.co.uk or by post to Cicerone, Juniper House, Murley Moss, Oxenholme Road, Kendal, LA9 7RL.

Register your book: To sign up to receive free updates, special offers and GPX files where available, register your book at www.cicerone.co.uk.

Front cover: The outwardly impressive Caernarfon Castle, which dominates the town (Stage 7)

CONTENTS

Symbols used on route maps

route		hostel	
alternative route		bike shop	
start point		railway station	
finish point		Tourist Information Centre	
route direction		castle or fort	
steep ascent or descent		priory	
very steep ascent or descent		point of interest	
		distance marker in miles	

GPX files

GPX files for all routes can be downloaded free at www.cicerone.co.uk/988/GPX.

Route maps are at a scale of 1cm = 200,000cm. All other maps, including town maps, vary. Please refer to the scale on the map.

ROUTE SUMMARY TABLES

A CIRCUIT OF WALES						
Stage	Start	End	Distance (miles/km)	Ascent (m)	Time*	Page
1	Cardiff	Mumbles	67/107	800	8–9	40
2	Mumbles	Tenby	73/117	1300	10–11	52
3	Tenby	Fishguard	64/102	1200	9–10	62
4	Fishguard	Aberaeron	55/88	1500	9–10	71
5	Aberaeron	Machynlleth	43/69	1100	7–8	79
6	Machynlleth	Porthmadog	48/77	1100	7–8	87
7	Porthmadog	Conwy	57/91	900	7–8	98
8	Conwy	Wrexham	65/104	800	7–8	112
9	Wrexham	Montgomery	50/80	900	6–7	121
10	Montgomery	Hay-on-Wye	48/77	1300	8–9	131
11	Hay-on-Wye	Chepstow	51/82	1300	8–9	138
12	Chepstow	Cardiff	36/58	200	4–5	151
			657/1051	**12,600**		

CROSS ROUTES							
Route	Start	via	End	Distance (miles/km)	Ascent (m)	Time*	Page
1	Wrexham	Corwen	Bangor	72/115	1800	11–12	160
2	Barmouth	Bala	Chirk	71/114	2000	12–13	171
3	Welshpool	Llanidloes	Machynlleth	54/87	1200	8–9	181
4	Aberystwyth	Rhayader	Knighton	71/114	1800	11–12	191
5	Fishguard	Crymych	Carmarthen	45/72	1200	7–8	200
6	Carmarthen	Brecon	Abergavenny	70/112	1300	10–11	207

* Time (hrs at 10mph/16kph + 400m/hr). See box 'Estimating times in hilly terrain' in the Introduction.

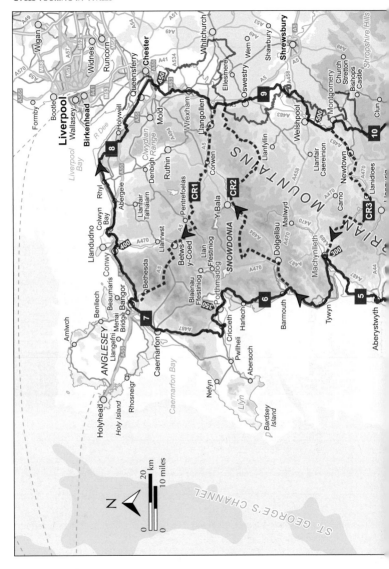

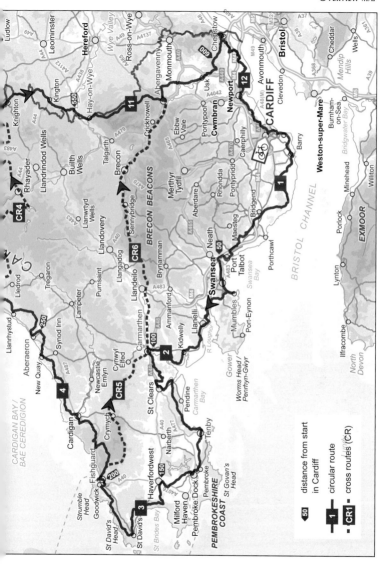

distance from start in Cardiff

1 circular route

CR1 cross routes (CR)

9

Ride planner from Cardiff

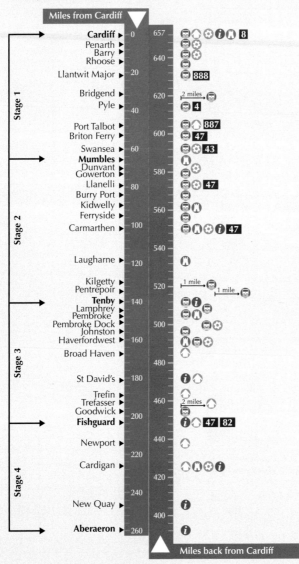

Miles from Cardiff ▼

Place	Miles from Cardiff	Miles back from Cardiff
Cardiff ▶	0	657
Penarth ▶		
Barry ▶		640
Rhoose ▶	20	
Llantwit Major ▶		
Bridgend ▶		620
Pyle ▶	40	
Port Talbot ▶		600
Briton Ferry ▶		
Swansea ▶	60	
Mumbles ▶		
Dunvant ▶		580
Gowerton ▶		
Llanelli ▶	80	
Burry Port ▶		
Kidwelly ▶		560
Ferryside ▶		
Carmarthen ▶	100	
		540
Laugharne ▶	120	
Kilgetty ▶		520
Pentrepoir ▶	140	
Tenby ▶		
Lamphrey ▶		500
Pembroke ▶		
Pembroke Dock ▶		
Johnston ▶	160	
Haverfordwest ▶		
Broad Haven ▶		480
St David's ▶	180	
Trefin ▶		460
Trefasser ▶		
Goodwick ▶	200	
Fishguard ▶		
Newport ▶		440
	220	
Cardigan ▶		420
	240	
New Quay ▶		400
Aberaeron ▶	260	

Stage 1, Stage 2, Stage 3, Stage 4

Miles back from Cardiff ▲

10

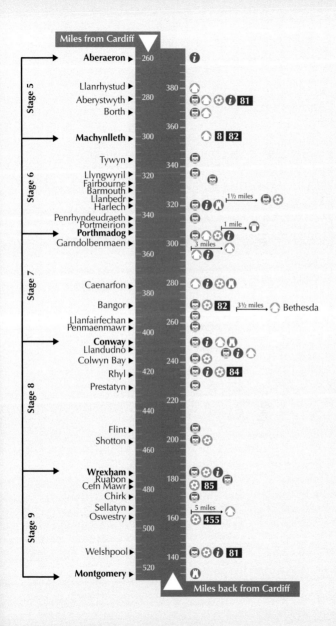

Miles from Cardiff ▼

Stage	Place	Miles	Miles (scale)

Stage 5
- Aberaeron ▸ 260
- Llanrhystud ▸ — 380
- Aberystwyth ▸ 280 — 81
- Borth ▸
- Machynlleth ▸ 300 — 8 82 — 360

Stage 6
- Tywyn ▸ — 340
- Llyngwyril ▸ 320
- Fairbourne ▸
- Barmouth ▸
- Llanbedr ▸ 320 — 1½ miles →
- Harlech ▸
- Penrhyndeudraeth ▸ — 340
- Portmeirion ▸
- Porthmadog ▸ — 1 mile →
- Garndolbenmaen ▸ — 360 — 3 miles →

Stage 7
- Caenarfon ▸ 280 — 380
- Bangor ▸ 82 — 3½ miles → Bethesda
- Llanfairfechan ▸ — 260
- Penmaenmawr ▸ — 400

Stage 8
- Conway ▸
- Llandudno ▸
- Colwyn Bay ▸ — 240
- Rhyl ▸ 420 — 84
- Prestatyn ▸ — 220
- — 440
- Flint ▸
- Shotton ▸ — 200 — 460

Stage 9
- Wrexham ▸ — 180
- Ruabon ▸
- Cefn Mawr ▸ 85
- Chirk ▸ — 480
- Sellatyn ▸
- Oswestry ▸ — 160 — 5 miles → — 455 — 500
- Welshpool ▸ — 140 — 81
- Montgomery ▸ — 520

△ Miles back from Cardiff

11

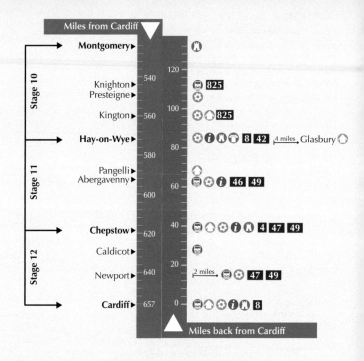

Miles from Cardiff ▽

Montgomery ▶ 🏰

	120	
Knighton ▶	540	🚲 **825**
Presteigne ▶		⊗
Kington ▶	560 — 100	⊗ ⌂ **825**
Hay-on-Wye ▶		⊗ 𝑖 🏰 🗪 **8** **42** ⊢4 miles⊣ Glasbury ⌂
	580 — 80	
Pangelli ▶		⌂
Abergavenny ▶		🚲 ⊗ 𝑖 **46** **49**
	600 — 60	
Chepstow ▶	620 — 40	🚲 ⌂ ⊗ 𝑖 🏰 **4** **47** **49**
Caldicot ▶		🚲
Newport ▶	640 — 20	⊢2 miles⊣→ 🚲 ⊗ **47** **49**
Cardiff ▶	657 — 0	🚲 ⌂ ⊗ 𝑖 🏰 **8**

△ **Miles back from Cardiff**

Stage 10 / Stage 11 / Stage 12

𝑖 Tourist information   ⌂ Hostel   🚲 Rail station   ⊗ Cycle shop
🗪 Antiquity   🏰 Castle
88 NCR link

Alternative Schedules

Miles from Cardiff ▼	7 DAYS	12 DAYS	15 DAYS
Cardiff ▶ —0			
—20	**Cardiff to Carmarthen** 103 miles 1300m ascent 8–9hr	**Cardiff to Mumbles** 67 miles 900m ascent 8–9hr	**Cardiff to Swansea** 61 miles 900m ascent 9–10hr
—40			
Swansea ▶ —60		**Mumbles to Tenby** 73 miles 1300m ascent 10–11hr	Swansea to Carmarthen 44 miles 580m ascent 7–8hr
Mumbles ▶			
—80			
	Carmarthen to Fishguard 101 miles 2000m ascent 10–11hr		**Carmarthen to Pembroke** 45 miles 1110m ascent 8–9hr
Carmarthen ▶ —100			
—120		**Tenby to Fishguard** 64 miles 1300m ascent 9–10hr	
Tenby ▶ —140			Pembroke to Trefin 43 miles 800m ascent 7–8hr
Pembroke ▶ —160			
—180			**Trefin to New Quay** 56 miles 1500m ascent 11–12hr
Trefin ▶ —200	**Fishguard to Aberystwth** 77 miles 2100m ascent 8–9hr	**Fishguard to Aberaeron** 55 miles 1600m ascent 9–10hr	
Fishguard ▶			
—220			
—240			New Quay to Borth 41 miles 1000m ascent 8–9hr
New Quay ▶ —260		Aberaeron to Machynlleth 43 miles 1100m ascent 7–8hr	
Aberaeron ▶			
Aberystwth ▶ —280	**Aberystwth to Caernarfon** 99 miles 2000m ascent 9–10hr		**Borth to Barmouth** 40 miles 800m ascent 7–8hr
Borth ▶ —300		Machynlleth to Porthmadog 48 miles 900m ascent 7–8hr	
Machynlleth ▶ —320			
		Porthmadog to Conway 57 miles 900m ascent 7–8hr	**Barmouth to Caernarfon** 50 miles 900m ascent 9–10hr
Barmouth ▶ —340			
Porthmadog ▶			
—360			
Caernarfon ▶ —380	**Caernarfon to Wrexham** 93 miles 1400m ascent 7–8hr	**Conway to Wrexham** 56 miles 800m ascent 7–8hr	**Caernarfon to Rhyl** 44 miles 450m ascent 9–10hr
Conway ▶ —400			
Rhyl ▶ —420			
—440			Rhyl to Wrexham 46 miles 770m ascent 6–7hr
—460			
Wrexham ▶ —480	**Wrexham to Hay-on-Wye** 98 miles 2200m ascent 9–10hr	**Wrexham to Montgomery** 50 miles 900m ascent 7–8hr	**Wrexham to Welshpool** 41 miles 770m ascent 7–8hr
—500			
Welshpool ▶ —520		Montgomery to Hay-on-Wye 48 miles 1300m ascent 8–9hr	Welshpool to Kington 45 miles 1300m ascent 9–10hr
Montgomery ▶			
—540			
Kington ▶ —560	**Hay-on-Wye to Cardiff** 87 miles 1500m ascent 7–8hr	**Hay-on-Wye to Chepstow** 51 miles 1300m ascent 8–9hr	Kington to Abergavenny 36 miles 800m ascent 6–7hr
Hay-on-Wye ▶ —580			
Abergavenny ▶ —600			Abergavenny to Chepstow 26 miles 700m ascent 5–6hr
—620		**Chepstow to Cardiff** 36 miles 200m ascent 4–5hr	**Chepstow to Cardiff** 36 miles 200m ascent 5–6hr
Chepstow ▶			
—640			
Cardiff ▶ —657			
	Time hr at 14mph (22kph) + 700m/hr	**Time hr** at 10mph (16kph) + 400m/hr	**Time hr** at 8mph (13kph) + 300m/hr

Cyclists on the Mawddach Trail near Penmaenpool (Cross route 2)

INTRODUCTION

Looking north towards Barmouth along the viaduct across the Mawddach Estuary (Stage 6)

When the Wales Coast Path was created in 2013, Wales became the first country in the world to have a dedicated footpath that follows its entire coastline. When coupled with the already famous Offa's Dyke National Trail from Chepstow to Prestatyn, it forms a 1030-mile walking route around the whole of the principality. This guidebook is for those who want to experience a similar circumnavigation of Wales by bike, following existing traffic-free paths and the quieter roads nearest the coast.

To make a circuit that can be comfortably ridden over a two-week holiday, the Gower Peninsula, Llyn Peninsula and Anglesey have been omitted, although there are suggestions in the text on how best to incorporate them into a tour. The resulting circuit provides 657 miles (1051km) of wonderful riding that starts on the waterfront in Cardiff, the capital city of Wales, and includes mile after mile of stunning coastal landscape before heading back south through the rolling marcher country along the border. You will ride past miles of golden sand along the south coast in Pembrokeshire, Britain's only coastal National Park; past the historic castles of Cardigan Bay; along the Menai Straight and through the seaside towns on the north coast, visiting some delightful towns and villages that benefit from being off the normal tourist itinerary.

Travelling through such wonderful countryside by bike is hugely satisfying for those who want to cover the miles quickly, as well as those preferring a more leisurely pace to watch wildlife and explore attractions along the way. There are plenty of pretty villages and interesting towns where you can top up your energy levels in local cafés and find interesting shops to replenish your supplies. These towns also provide a good choice of overnight accommodation and places for dinner, although you may need to leave the route to find exactly what you're looking for. Add to that an impressive collection of castles, industrial archaeology, churches, chapels and prehistoric sites along the route and you have a ride that you will remember for a very long time.

The magnificent red kite is now a common sight in many parts of Central Wales (Image authorised for common usage)

Kidwelly Castle from the bank of Gwendraeth Fach (Stage 2)

WELSH CHAPELS: THE OTHER ICONIC BUILDINGS OF WALES

Apart from its magnificent castles, Wales' other iconic buildings are its chapels, and you will see hundreds of examples while cycling through the country. Up until the Toleration Act 1689 was passed, it was illegal for dissenters to meet for worship, so many congregations met secretly in remote houses and barns. But from the end of the 17th century until the early 20th century, congregations built around 10,000 chapels, often financing their construction with loans that took decades to pay off. Initially, the chapels were quite plain but once the congregations started to commission architects, the chapels began to reflect the height of fashion, particularly during the later Victorian era when it became quite common to amalgamate all manner of influences into ornate gable end walls. Many were also rebuilt or remodelled to accommodate a growing congregation, often through the addition of a gallery that had been cleverly allowed for in the original design.

Some still maintain a thriving congregation but many have been converted for residential or commercial use, such as Libanus Chapel in Borth, which has been turned into a cinema and bistro. Others stand empty and strangely silent, waiting for someone to rescue them from creeping dereliction and potential demolition. See www.welshchapels.org for further information and an interactive map that provides more details about each of the chapels along the route.

The page opposite shows six chapels of different styles that you will pass while riding around Wales.

- Henllan Baptist Chapel (top left), in the Vale of Eywas on Stage 11, was built in 1865 in the Vernacular style with a single door on the gable end.

- Blaen-y-Cefn Methodist Chapel (top right), just north of Cardigan on Stage 4, was built in 1808. It was rebuilt in 1837 in the Simple Round-Headed style with separate doors for men and women along the long wall. Traditionally, the men sat in the pews to the right of the minister and the women and children sat in the pews to his left, with the interior layout designed so the minister could see everyone.

- Llanfairfechan Methodist Chapel (centre left) on Stage 9 was built sometime before 1897 using corrugated iron. It is still in use and is known locally as 'Capel Sinc'.

- Bryn Seion Methodist Chapel (centre right), near the Pontcysyllte Aqueduct on Stage 9, was built in the Classical style in 1902 using locally made red brick. The Grade II listed building has been sympathetically converted into a cycle-friendly café and bistro.

• Seion Welsh Independent Chapel (bottom left), situated in Baker Street, Aberystwyth on Stage 5, was built in the Italianate Classical style in 1876 by the Welsh-born architect Richard Owens (1831–1891), whose Liverpool-based practice was responsible for 250–300 chapels, largely in North Wales. Owens was by no means the most prolific of the known chapel architects, though, as his contemporary, the largely self-taught Welsh Independent minister, Thomas Thomas (1817–1888) is reputed to have played a part in the building, restoration or extension of some 1000 chapels throughout Wales. It is thought that he delivered the first sermon in each of the chapels he was involved with. However, after an illustrious career he was forced into semi-retirement when it was revealed that he owned almost 40 properties around Swansea that were used as brothels.

• Zion English Presbyterian Church (bottom right), located in Mansel Street, Carmarthen on Stage 2, was built in the Classical style in 1850 by the architect RG Thomas (1820–1883) of Newport. It remains in use and is now a Grade II listed building.

As the route is circular you can start and finish your tour at any point along the way. Detailed information is provided on the rail services you can use to get to and from the towns chosen for the start and finish of each stage, most of which are on the rail network. Although it is always best to follow the advice of the particular train operator, taking bikes on trains in Wales is typically far easier than in other parts of the UK, so you can leave the car at home.

Convenient access by rail also means you can split a circumnavigation across two or more tours starting and finishing at stations on or near the route. The additional cross routes, which all start and finish at towns served by rail, mean you can also plan shorter tours that are easy to get to without using a vehicle. A number of shorter tours are suggested in this guide, but you can easily use the detailed information provided to plan your own route to fit the time you have available.

WHY CYCLE AROUND WALES?

A circumnavigation of Wales covers the entire country from the industrial south to the sea cliffs of Pembrokeshire, passing through wild

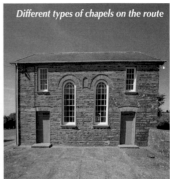

Different types of chapels on the route

GEORGE BORROW: WALES'S GREATEST TRAVELLER

On the morning of 29 July 1854 the Victorian travel writer, George Borrow, set out from Chester and walked on a circuitous route around Wales, while his wife and stepdaughter used coaches and the newly opened railways to hop between inns along the way. Despite his 51 years and his snow-white hair, Borrow was upright and athletic and would continue to ride horses and swim outdoors into his seventies, also undertaking long walks at a brisk pace that lasted for many weeks. He recounted his travels in the book *Wild Wales*, which remains in print over 150 years after it was first published in 1862. Throughout his life Borrow had three main interests: languages, legends and Romany gypsies, and he was able to indulge himself in all three during his walking holiday in Wales.

Before his late marriage, Borrow had worked overseas for the Bible Society and was fluent in Russian, Spanish and Portuguese. But many of the other languages he claimed to speak he learnt from books, so his understanding of their grammar and pronunciation was probably rudimentary at best. He learnt Welsh by comparing a translation of John Milton's *Paradise Lost* by the Welsh antiquarian and grammarian William Owen Pughe (1759–1835) with the original English verse. He supplemented this with some oral coaching from 'Taffy' Lloyd, a Welsh-born ostler employed by William Simpson at the Norwich solicitors where he had served a legal apprenticeship while in his teens. Taffy's tuition was not the best, and 30 years later when Borrow got to try out his Welsh on locals, those in North Wales thought he must originate from South Wales and those in South Wales thought he must originate from North Wales, while others thought he was a Breton.

Borrow died in 1881, four years before the introduction of the safety bicycle, which is now recognized as the catalyst in cycling becoming a popular pastime. But if they had arrived on the scene during his lifetime, I feel sure he would have ridden one, delighting in the speed with which he could travel and the fact that it was all due to his own physical effort. I considered following the route Borrow travelled in *Wild Wales* by bike as it would be fascinating to compare what he saw and described with what can be seen today, using the early Ordnance Survey maps to follow his route and Victorian censuses and parish records to identify the people he met. However this is hardly feasible as many of the rutted roads that Borrow walked along are now busy trunk roads, but I will share his observations of some of the places he visited in 1854 in the route descriptions.

mountains and along green valleys, where some of the events that shaped Wales took place. In addition to the beautiful, varied landscape, there is great satisfaction in doing a ride that circumnavigates a country, taking in its history and industrial heritage as well as the less-visited and sparsely populated areas along the border.

The route makes extensive use of traffic-free, shared-use paths, particularly through the cities and towns along the south and north coasts, and uses waymarked National Cycle Routes that run along the coast or down the border wherever possible. This makes route-finding much easier. However, inevitably, there are some sections where you need to follow the detailed route description diligently and/or use a satnav.

HOW TOUGH IS IT?

This circuit of Wales can be ridden as a leisure activity or as a challenge, and this guidebook provides schedules for both types of rider. There are some hilly sections, particularly along the west coast and the border. However, the gradients are never extreme, with even the Gospel Pass above Hay-on-Wye, which is the highest road in Wales, snaking steadily uphill for 5 miles at an average gradient of 5.5%.

WHICH DIRECTION TO RIDE

Because of the prevailing south-westerly winds that sometimes rip up the exposed west coast, it is usually easier to ride a circuit of Wales in a clockwise direction as described in this guidebook. Riding

A cyclist nears the top of the Gospel Pass after the long climb for Hay-on-Wye (Stage 11)

Looking north along the Promenade at Aberystwyth (Stage 5)

in this direction also means you quickly escape the predominantly urban landscape between Cardiff and Swansea. However, you may decide to ride the route in the opposite direction, in which case you will need to adapt the directions in the route descriptions.

SELECTING A SCHEDULE

Inevitably, the 12 stages of this guidebook will not necessarily coincide with your personal itinerary, which will depend on the amount of time you have available, your daily mileage and whether you wish to visit attractions along the way. If you want a more relaxed schedule, allow more time for the more undulating west coast and the southern section of the English border.

The availability of accommodation will also determine where your days begin and end, which could be at places before the end of a stage, into the following stage or perhaps somewhere off the route altogether.

When planning your ride:
• first decide how many days you can spare or need,
• then use the alternative schedules to identify roughly where each day will ideally begin and end.
• Identify the most convenient accommodation that suits your budget. This may mean amending your initial schedule so be prepared to be flexible, perhaps enjoying a night in a B&B if there are no hostels nearby and vice versa.
• Book your accommodation and finalize your schedule. You will have more choice of where to stay if you book your accommodation well in advance of your departure date.

You can combine the cross routes with sections of the circular route to plan your own itinerary. The suggested tours are categorized as short, medium and long, but you can take them at your own pace.

Short Tours (2–3 days)

**Around North Wales: 144 miles/
230km with 3000m of ascent**
This circular tour crosses North Wales
from the border through the dramatic
Snowdonia Mountains before turning
back along the coast to return to the
start at Wrexham. It is easily accessed
by rail and there is plenty of accommodation to choose from throughout
the route.

**Tour of Pembrokeshire: 146 miles/
234km with 3300m of ascent**
This wonderful short tour around the
spectacular coast of Pembrokeshire is
easy to reach using the train network,
with direct services from many mainland stations.

**Across and back: 156 miles/250km
with 3650m of ascent**
This tour runs from the border to the
coast and back again through some of
the less-visited parts of Wales. Again,

Around North Wales: 144 miles/230km with 3000m of ascent				
Start	**Route**	**Finish**	**Travelling time**	**% total**
Wrexham	Cross Route 1	Bangor	6–7hr	30%
Bangor	Stage 7 (part)	Conwy	2–3hr	45%
Conwy	Stage 8	Wrexham	11–12hr	100%

Tour of Pembrokeshire: 146 miles/234km with 3300m of ascent				
Start	**Route**	**Finish**	**Travelling time**	**% total**
Carmarthen	Stage 2 (part)	Tenby	5–6hr	25%
Tenby	Stage 3	Fishguard	9–10hr	66%
Fishguard	Cross Route 5	Carmarthen	7–8hr	100%

Across and back: 156 miles/250km with 3650m of ascent				
Start	**Route**	**Finish**	**Travelling time**	**% total**
Welshpool	Stage 9 (part)	Montgomery	1–2hr	6%
Montgomery	Stage 10 (part)	Knighton	3–4hr	18%
Knighton	Cross Route 4 (reversed)	Aberystwyth	11–12hr	54%
Aberystwyth	Stage 5 (part)	Machynlleth	3–4hr	71%
Machynlleth	Cross Route 3 (reverse)	Welshpool	8–9hr	100%

it is easily accessed via the national rail network – and you may also wish to take the train between Aberystwyth or Tywyn and Machynlleth to avoid a particularly busy stretch of the A487. See Stage 5 for further details.

Medium tours (4–5days)

Around the heartlands: 171 miles/ 273km with 7100m of ascent

This circuit has considerable variety, including the well-surfaced canal towpath between Welshpool and Newtown, the high mountain road between Llanidloes and Machynlleth, the seaside at Barmouth and a high-level traverse of the Berwyn Mountains back to the start.

Around the Welsh Valleys: 232 miles/ 371km with 3500m of ascent

This easily accessible tour takes in the South Wales coast, where much of the route follows a shared-use path, returning on quiet lanes along the northern edge of the Brecon Beacons.

Through the high hills: 218 miles/ 349km with 5040m of ascent

This more demanding short tour passes through Snowdonia before turning south down the more gentle west coast, returning over the Berwyn Mountains. Plenty of accommodation is available in the resorts and coastal towns, and you may wish to take a rest day before tackling the more strenuous ascent on the return leg.

Around the heartlands: 171 miles/273km with 7100m of ascent				
Start	**Route**	**Finish**	**Travelling time**	**% total**
Welshpool	Cross Route 3	Machynlleth	8–9hr	30%
Machynlleth	Stage 6 (part)	Barmouth	3–4hr	42%
Barmouth	Cross Route 3	Chirk	12–13hr	84%
Chirk	Stage 9 (part)	Welshpool	4–5hr	100%

Around the Welsh Valleys: 232 miles/371km with 3500m of ascent				
Start	**Route**	**Finish**	**Travelling time**	**% total**
Cardiff	Stage 1	Mumbles	8–9hr	24%
Mumbles	Stage 2 (part)	Carmarthen	5–6hr	41%
Carmarthen	Cross Route 6	Abergavenny	10–11hr	70%
Abergavenny	Stage 11 (part)	Chepstow	5–6hr	86%
Chepstow	Stage 12	Cardiff	4–5hr	100%

Through the high hills: 218 miles/349km with 5040m of ascent				
Start	Route	Finish	Travelling time	% total
Wrexham	Cross Route 1	Bangor	6–7 hr	22%
Bangor	Stage 7 (part reversed)	Porthmadog	5–6hr	41%
Porthmadog	Stage 6 (part reversed)	Barmouth	3–4hr	53%
Barmouth	Cross Route 2	Chirk	12–13hr	94%
Chirk	Stage 9 (part reversed)	Wrexham	1–2hr	100%

Longer tours (6–7 days)
The following three tours are ideal for those who can only get away for a week. They are all easily accessible by rail, and there are plenty of opportunities to resort to the train should you need to make up lost time.

Loop of North Wales: 348 miles/ 556km with 7100m of ascent
This is the easiest of the longer tours as it avoids the higher mountains.

Loop around Central Wales: 422 miles/ 675km with 10,000m of ascent
This week-long tour takes in the less-populated parts of Wales, which is ideal for those wanting to get away from it all.

Loop around South Wales: 472 miles/ 755km with 9200m of ascent
This longer tour can either be ridden fast over a hard week or taken at a much more leisurely pace over two weeks.

Loop of North Wales: 348 miles/556km with 7100m of ascent				
Start	Route	Finish	Travelling time	% total
Wrexham	Stage 9	Montgomery	6–7hr	13%
Montgomery	Stage 10 (part)	Knighton	4–5hr	23%
Knighton	Cross Route 4 (reversed)	Aberystwyth	11–12hr	46%
Aberystwyth	Stage 5 (part)	Machynlleth	3–4hr	54%
Machynlleth	Stage 6	Porthmadog	7–8hr	69%
Porthmadog	Stage 7	Conwy	7–8hr	84%
Conwy	Stage 8	Wrexham	7–8hr	100%

Loop around Central Wales: 422 miles/675km with 10,000m of ascent				
Start	**Route**	**Finish**	**Travelling time**	**% total**
Welshpool	Stage 9 (part)	Montgomery	1–2hr	3%
Montgomery	Stage 10	Hay-on-Wye	8–9hr	15%
Hay-on-Wye	Stage 11 (part)	Abergavenny	3–4hr	21%
Abergavenny	Cross Route 6 (reverse)	Carmarthen	10–11hr	39%
Carmarthen	Cross Route 5 (reverse)	Fishguard	7–8hr	46%
Fishguard	Stage 4	Aberaeron	9–10hr	59%
Aberaeron	Stage 5	Machynlleth	7–8hr	70%
Machynlleth	Stage 6 (part)	Barmouth	3–4hr	76%
Barmouth	Cross Route 2	Chirk	12–13hr	93%
Chirk	Stage 9 (part)	Welshpool	4–5hr	100%

Loop around South Wales: 472 miles/755km with 9200m of ascent				
Start	**Route**	**Finish**	**Travelling time**	**% total**
Cardiff	Stage 1	Mumbles	8–9hr	13%
Mumbles	Stage 2	Tenby	5–6hr	21%
Tenby	Stage 3	Fishguard	10–11hr	37%
Fishguard	Stage 4	Aberaeron	9–10hr	51%
Aberaeron	Stage 5 (part)	Aberystwyth	3–4hr	56%
Aberystwyth	Cross Route 4	Knighton	11–12hr	73%
Knighton	Stage 10 (part)	Hay-on-Wye	4–5hr	80%
Hay-on-Wye	Stage 11	Chepstow	8–9hr	93%
Chepstow	Stage 12	Cardiff	4–5hr	100%

GETTING THERE

Many local cyclists will happily add an extra day or two to either end of their tour and make use of the National Cycle Network (NCN) to get to the route and back. But others from further afield, and those pressed for time, will undoubtedly need another form of transport. Unless you are riding in a big group or on a tandem, the easiest way to access the route is by train, as Cardiff, Chepstow and Holyhead are all on the national rail network. Similarly, there are a number of stations along the route, so you can easily split the ride into sections. See 'By rail' below for further details.

If you are riding as a group you may be able to commandeer someone to drop you at one end and collect you from the other. Some lucky groups may have their support vehicle stay with them to move luggage between stops and provide catering support.

TRAVEL

For details on all public transport journeys throughout the UK, including local bus services, tel 0871 200 2233 www.traveline.info or www.traveline.cymru.

By rail
There are numerous stations where you can start or finish your bike ride around Wales as detailed in the notes below. But for general information on travel by rail tel 08457 484 950 www.nationalrail.co.uk

Cardiff Central Station, where the route description of the circular tour starts and finishes, provides direct trains to stations in West Wales and most parts of the UK. Great Western Railway provides services between the south of England and Cardiff, Swansea and beyond. They have space for bicycles on most trains but ask that you reserve your bike space when booking your tickets online, at a ticket office or by calling 0345 7000 125. See www.gwr.com for details.

All correctly ticketed awaiting the morning train

Railway stations on or adjacent to the route

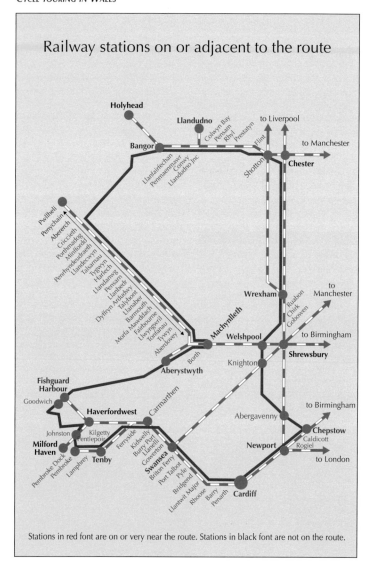

Stations in red font are on or very near the route. Stations in black font are not on the route.

Aberystwyth, Barmouth, Criccieth, Porthmadog, Harlech, and other stations on the Cambrian Coast Line, are close to the circular route and provide services via Machynlleth to Shrewsbury and Birmingham, with connections to most other parts of the UK.

Bangor Station, on the North Wales Coast Line, provides trains to Chester and Cardiff, with connections to most other parts of the UK.

Trafnidiaeth Cymru/Transport For Wales runs local and commuter services along the north coast tfwrail. wales. The train company provides bike space on all of their services except during peak hours on some Valleys and Cardiff Local Routes. They recommend that you make a reservation as far in advance as possible and reserve a cycle space at the time of booking. You can do this at any staffed national rail station or by calling their telesales office on 0870 9000 773. See tfwrail.wales for further details.

Virgin Trains runs mainline services to and from Holyhead and provides special bike storage areas with space for up to 4 bikes, but you will need to reserve a space for your bike before you travel. The service is free and reservations can be made at any booking office or by calling 0344 556 5650. On the day of travel, collect your bike reservation coupons at a FastTicket machine at the station by keying in your FastTicket reference number and the number of the bank card you used to make the booking.

Then give yourself a minimum of 10 minutes to contact a member of the Virgin platform staff, who will help you load your bicycle. Once aboard, inform the Train Manager that you are travelling with a bicycle, and he will help you disembark at your destination station. It sounds complicated, but it seems to work even though local staff may not be entirely familiar with the process. See www.virgintrains. co.uk for details.

Wrexham General Station is on the Shrewsbury to Chester line, with connections to most other parts of the UK; visit tfwrail.wales for further details.

Abergavenny Station is on the Newport to Hereford line.

Chepstow Station is on the Newport to Birmingham line, with connections to most other parts of the UK; visit tfwrail.wales for further details.

By bus
National Express, Britain's only scheduled coach network, says it will carry dismantled and folding bicycles if space is available, provided the bikes are suitably packed. However, the coach company also states that carrying a bike on a service does not guarantee that it will carry it on any subsequent service. As this provides cyclists with no reassurance that their bike will be carried, let alone any advice on what to do with the transit box when they start cycling, the company may as well say no.

Built in 1897 as the headquarters for the Bute Dock Company, the Pierhead Building in Cardiff Bay is now used by the National Assembly for Wales

The same goes for the TrawsCambria service between South and North Wales, which involves a number of stages each operated by a different bus company. Not all of the companies carry bikes, and you are advised to contact each operator individually. A further deterrent is that the journey takes 11 hours. For more information visit www.trawscymru.info.

By air

Cardiff airport, near the southern end of the route, provides international and domestic services. Anglesey airport, near the northern end of the route, only provides a twice daily service to and from Cardiff. Alternative airports include Manchester, Liverpool, Birmingham and Bristol, although arriving at any one of these airports still leaves you a journey of 100 miles or more,

necessitating using public transport or hiring a car.

If you are planning to fly with your bike, you should contact your airline and make a reservation when you book your seat. The airline will charge you for carrying your bike and will ask that you follow their packing instructions; these typically include turning and locking the handlebars parallel with the frame, removing the pedals and front wheel and attaching them to the frame and deflating the tyres before placing the bike in a carrying bag or transit box.

By ferry

Stena Line operates between Dublin or Dun Laoghaire and Holyhead; visit www.stenaline.co.uk for details.

Irish Ferries Line operates between Dublin and Holyhead. Visit www.irishferries.co.uk for details.

FIRST AND LAST NIGHTS IN CARDIFF

Cardiff is easily accessible by rail and there is even an extension of NCN 8, which runs for 2 miles from the main station to the start of the route in Cardiff Bay. There is also a huge choice of accommodation, from five-star hotels to ultra-modern hostels with private rooms and internal bike storage. As Wales's capital city, Cardiff is home to the National Museum, which houses the national art, natural history and geology collections, as well as temporary exhibitions. But there are plenty of other attractions, such as Cardiff Castle and Cardiff Bay, world-famous sporting venues, top-class entertainment and quality shopping – making it great place to spend an extra night.

WHEN TO RIDE

The best time to go is between April and October when the days are longer and the weather is at its best. But even then you may experience inclement days so always check the weather forecast before you set out, so you will know whether to keep your waterproof at the top of your pack and wear your overshoes from the start. But if you are struggling, and the weather forecast is atrocious, consider taking the train or see whether a local taxi service can move you and your bike along the route. You can always come back and ride the section you missed another time.

ACCOMMODATION

While some cycle tourists prefer to camp, days of repeatedly ascending 1000m or more are unlikely to be pleasurable with heavy luggage. This guide makes maximum use of hostels and bunkhouses along or near the route (though also lists a selection of cycle-friendly hotels and B&Bs – see Appendix B), but if you prefer additional comforts you will find information on a variety of accommodation to suit most pockets at the Welsh Tourist Board, www.visitwales.com. You may not be able to get exactly what you

Heading west towards St Donat's on a perfectly sunny day (Stage 1)

want at the start or finish of each of stage, so you may have to curtail your day before the end of a stage, ride further into the next stage or temporarily leave the route.

Hostels are always busy during the summer months, and those in the more popular locations can be full at weekends and sometimes even in the depths of winter, so it pays to book early. The Youth Hostel Association, www.yha.org.uk, has a number of hostels in Wales, and there is an increasing number of independent hostels – see www.independenthostelguide.co.uk for details.

It is worth seeking out Visit Wales's star-graded B&Bs, guest houses and hotels enrolled in their Cyclists Welcome scheme, which provides drying facilities, bike storage and other services. Whatever you choose, if you want to arrive early to drop off your bike and go sightseeing, or anticipate arriving late due to an unforeseen delay, it is only courteous to ring ahead and let them know.

WHAT TO TAKE

The plethora of accommodation and the high number of cycle shops along the route mean you can keep the bike as light as possible. Here are my tips to lighten your load:

- Think layers and add-ons rather than alternatives.
- Use drying facilities to rinse through cycling gear and other clothing every evening.
- Choose leisurewear, such as long-sleeved T-shirts, that can also be an extra layer for chilly days.
- Share tools and accessories.

Waiting to check in to a wonderfully situated hostel at St David's (Stage 3)

A popular cycle café in Llantwit Major that goes the extra mile by providing cycle locks for customers to shackle their bikes to nearby railings

- Buy travel-sized toiletries and give shaving a miss for the week.
- Make do with a smartphone and leave all other electronics at home.
- Only carry one feed-bottle – it'll be plenty.
- Use accommodation with secure storage and leave the heavy bike lock at home.
- But always wear a helmet as riding without one is irresponsible.

Adopting such guidelines produces the kit list shown in Appendix D, which totals 5–7kg for summer tours and 7–9kg during winter. Having reduced your kit as much as possible, you should be able to fit it easily into a pair of panniers or a set of seat and frame packs.

PREPARING YOUR BIKE

Other than for a very short section on the old coach road between Newbridge-on-Wye and Rhayader, the road surface is remarkably good so you can ride the route on a road bike, a mountain bike or a hybrid/city bike. However, there are some things that you can do to make your ride more comfortable:

- Leave your best carbon frame and carbon wheels at home.
- Use tyres that are 28mm or wider as they will be more comfortable, especially over the short sections of gravel track that are occasionally encountered.
- Swap mountain bike tyres for lower profile urban tyres, which

require less effort and provide a quieter ride.

- Fit a cassette with a 30-, 32- or 34-tooth sprocket to make it easier to climb hills.

- Fit bar ends to straight handlebars so you have more choice for resting tired hands.

- Fit a bell, which is essential for negotiating pedestrians on shared-use paths.

Whatever you choose, It is always advisable to have your bike serviced a couple of weeks before your trip, allowing sufficient time for any worn parts to be replaced and run-in before your departure. There are plenty of cycle shops on or near the route, see Appendix A for details.

EATING

Cycling is strenuous so keep your energy reserves topped up by eating frequently, otherwise you will soon 'hit the wall' and feel tired and demotivated. However, it is best to avoid a full breakfast as it will weigh heavy for most of the morning. Get into the routine of eating little and often rather than waiting until you feel hungry, as by then it is frequently too late.

Many cyclists rely on things such as sandwiches, fruitcake, cereal bars and fruit. That's not to say, you should ignore the region's many inns and cafés; but err on the side of caution and stick to energy-giving snacks and pastries rather than a full midday meal.

CYCLING DOS AND DON'TS

- Be considerate to others on shared-use paths, particularly to children and dogs, which can often behave unpredictably. Ring your bell or call out to pass – and always say thank you.

- Although you can legally ride two abreast, quickly move into single file on minor roads always giving a cheery wave to thank considerate drivers.

- Scan ahead for hazards, such as road furniture, grit and livestock detritus.

- Avoid the green mossy strip along the centre of tree-lined roads as it may be slippery.

- Always park your bike in a prominent position and secure it with a 'café lock' when you go exploring.

- Ride across cattle grids square-on, standing on the pedals with your knees bent and you will hardly notice them.

- Always use hand signals to make your intentions clear to others.

10 FOODS TO TRY IN WALES

- Bara brith (speckled bread) is a Welsh version of tea loaf enriched with dried fruit and mixed spices, usually served sliced and buttered.

- Glamorgan sausage (*selsig morgannwg*), which is traditionally made from Caerphilly cheese, leeks, breadcrumbs and spices, was popular during World War II when meat was in short supply.

- Cawl, often said to be the national dish of Wales, is a broth made from meat, potatoes, swedes, carrots and other seasonal vegetables, such as leeks.

- Thought to have originated in the Welsh Valleys in the 18th century, Welsh rarebit is cheese on toast, sometimes mixed with onions, egg and milk and seasoned with salt and pepper.

- Crempog is a pancake made with flour, buttermilk, eggs, vinegar and salted butter traditionally served on Shrove Tuesday and other days of celebration, such as birthdays.

- By the time you finish the ride you will have seen thousands on the hillsides, so why not try Welsh lamb close to where it is reared.

- Look out for the oggie – a D-shaped pasty made with lamb and leeks.

- Welsh cakes are baked circular delights spiced with cinnamon and nutmeg and dusted in caster sugar.

- Laverbread (*bara lawr*) is an edible seaweed usually served with toast or alongside bacon and eggs for breakfast.

- Some quality craft beers are produced on or near the route: Brains, Bullmastiff and Crafty Devil (Cardiff); Vale of Glamorgan Brewery I (Barry); Tomos & Lilford Brewery (Llantwit Major); Borough Brewery and Neath Ales (Neath); Boss Brewing, Tomos Watkins and Mumbles Brewery (Swansea); Preseli Brewery (Tenby); Bluestone Brewing (Cilgwyn, Pembrokeshire); Penlon Cottage Brewery (New Quay); Purple Moose (Porthmadog); Great Orme Brewery and Wild Horse Brewing (Llandudno); Monty's Brewery (Montgomery) and Tiny Rebel (Newport).

A road cyclist climbing the Nant Ffrancon Pass with Tryfan on the skyline (Cross route 1)

PHONES AND WI-FI

Although mobile coverage is generally good, phone users in Wales have the least access to 4G networks in the UK, so you may not be able to post your photos straight to social media when riding through the Cambrian Mountains in Mid Wales. However, many cafés and pubs provide free Wi-Fi access so you should not be offline for too long.

EMERGENCIES

You may encounter few fellow cyclists along some of the more remote stages in Mid Wales, so it pays to be prepared for problems or emergencies. Should you have a good mobile phone signal, you can telephone the emergency services by dialling 999 or 112. However, it is always wise to let someone know your plans, particularly across the more remote hills between Machynlleth and Dolgellau on Cross route 3.

WAYMARKING

Where NCN routes are followed, they are generally well signed with fingerposts at major junctions and small blue repeater signs along the way. It can occasionally become confusing when signage for local routes takes precedent, when another NCN route briefly follows the same course or when signs are hidden behind undergrowth or temporarily misplaced. So it pays to be attentive at junctions, checking as you approach a junction and as you ride away from it to see if there is signage for riders going in the opposite direction.

Having the route downloaded on to a GPS, so that you get a reassuring beep at every junction, is also reassuring but not a necessity. However, GPS devices also have a nasty habit of losing satellite connection along the extensive tree-lined sections of the route, and you may need to carry a power pack to top up the battery while riding.

MAPS

This book is designed to be small enough to carry with you and includes linear maps that are entirely adequate for following the route. However, they do not show much on either side of the route, such as where your overnight accommodation is located, so it is advisable to carry separate maps, such as those in the Ordnance Survey 1:50,000 Landranger Series for such purposes.

USING THIS GUIDE

Although the circumnavigation is organised into 12 stages, it is most likely you will choose to use one of the suggested alternative schedules or work out your own itinerary. Each stage starts and finishes at a location where there is a selection of different types of accommodation and good local facilities. At the beginning of each stage, an information box summarises the practical details associated with the stage, including the start and finish points (with grid references), distance, total ascent and numbers of the relevant Ordnance Survey map sheets should you wish to explore. An estimation of the time required to complete the stage is provided, although this will of course vary considerably according to fitness and the prevailing weather. Details of attractions and services along the stage are also provided.

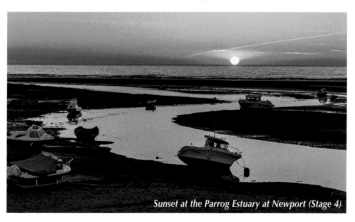

Sunset at the Parrog Estuary at Newport (Stage 4)

The route shown on the accompanying 1:200,000 maps is then described in detail with features that appear on the maps highlighted in **bold** in the text. Detailed maps show the route where it is sometimes difficult to find the way back to the route after taking a break to explore. Distances shown in brackets in the route description are the cumulative distance from the start of the stage and the distance still to ride to the end of the stage.

GPX tracks

GPX tracks for the routes in this guidebook are available to download free at www.cicerone.co.uk/988/GPX. A GPS device is an excellent aid to navigation, but you should also carry a map and, essentially, know how to use it. GPX files are provided in good faith, but neither the author nor the publisher accepts responsibility for their accuracy.

ESTIMATING TIMES IN HILLY TERRAIN

Estimating how long a ride will take when it involves a significant amount of climbing is notoriously difficult. Hillwalkers use Naismith's Rule, which allows 1 hour for every 3 miles (5km) covered in distance plus 1 hour for every 2000ft (600m) of ascent. Because there is considerable variation between the speed and climbing abilities of a committed club cyclist and a leisure cyclist, there is no comparable benchmark in cycling. However, the basic principle still applies.

Total time = time to cover the distance + time spent ascending

The Italian physician and cycling coach Michele Ferrari developed the term *velocità ascensionale media* (VAM) to refer to the average speed of ascent. VAM is usually expressed as metres per hour (m/h) and winners of mountain stages in grand tours typically climb at more than 1500m/h, while most club cyclists are capable of climbing somewhere in the range of 700 and 900m/h.

In this book much more modest values have been used for VAM, with estimated times based on 10mph (16kph) plus 400m/h. So a stage of 50 miles that involves 800m of ascent is estimated to take roughly 7 hours.

To get an estimate of your own VAM, first assess your average speed on the flat and then record your times for a number of measured climbs and see what number best fits. But if all of this is too much for you, just use the rule of thumb that 5 miles in the hills takes about as long as 8 miles on the flat.

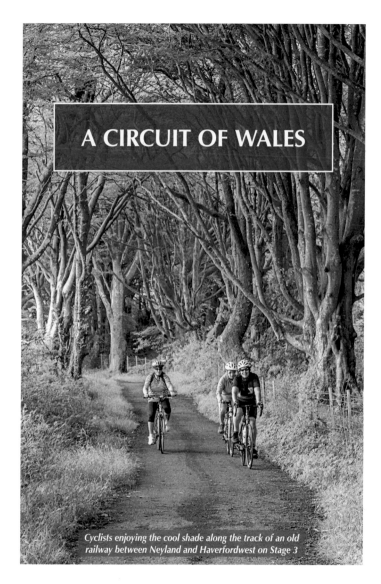

A CIRCUIT OF WALES

Cyclists enjoying the cool shade along the track of an old railway between Neyland and Haverfordwest on Stage 3

STAGE 1
Cardiff to Mumbles

Start	Cardiff Central Railway Station (ST 184 759)
Finish	Below Oystermouth Castle, Mumbles (SS 616 885)
Distance	67 miles (107km)
Ascent	800m
Time	8–9hr
OS maps	OS Landranger 171, 170 and 159
Refreshments	Lots of places to stop at along the route
Accommodation	Plenty of accommodation of all types in towns, including hostels in Cardiff and just off route before Port Talbot

Wales can claim to be the world's first industrialized country with more people in the 1851 population census working in industry than in agriculture. This stage passes through the coastal towns that were once the powerhouses of industry – as well as through the local seaside resorts that grew to provide recreation for the workers. The route makes use of NCN trails wherever possible and follows many miles of local shared-use paths. The final 13 miles around Swansea Bay are entirely traffic free.

Penarth was a popular holiday destination during the Victorian era when it was promoted as 'The Garden by the Sea'.

Head south following the blue signs for local route 4 down **Lloyd George Avenue** towards Cardiff Bay. Ride through **Roald Dahl Plass** past the Wales Millennium Centre, around the bay and across Cardiff Barricade to **Penarth** (3/64 miles). ◄

Out in the **Bristol Channel** are the islands of Flat Holm, which traditionally was part of Wales, and Steep Holm, which belonged to England. Once they were fortified to defend shipping using local ports but both are now protected nature reserves and sites of special scientific interest.

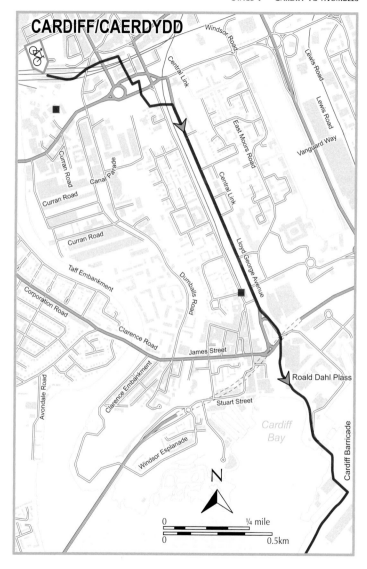

CARDIFF/CAERDYDD

Windsor Road

Central Link

Lewis Road

Lewis Road

Vanguard Way

East Moors Road

Central Link

Curran Road

Canal Parade

Lloyd George Avenue

Curran Road

Curran Road

Taff Embankment

Corporation Road

Dumballs Road

Clarence Road

James Street

Roald Dahl Plass

Clarence Embankment

Stuart Street

Avondale Road

Cardiff Bay

Windsor Esplanade

Cardiff Barricade

N

0 ¼ mile

0 0.5km

Parked up below the impressive steel and copper front of Wales Millennium Centre (Canolfan Mileniwm Cymru) in Cardiff Bay

Turn right at the roundabout at the end of Penarth Portway and follow NCN 88 alongside the marina before turning left up the serpentine shared-use path that provides an easy ascent to the town centre. Ride through the town centre and past the railway station to join a largely traffic-free path that ends at Cosmeston Drive.

Turn right, then left and follow a shared-use path alongside the **B4267**. Ride through **Sully** (8/59 miles) and then turn left along the **A4055** using the sections of shared-use path that have been created so far. Go straight on at the next roundabout, cross the carriageway and follow a shared-use path alongside Ffordd-Y-Mileniwm through Barry Docks (11/56 miles). There are plenty of

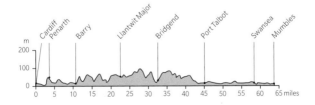

signs for the Wales Coast Path along this section of the route but none for NCN 88. However, as long as you keep heading west along the shared-use path, you cannot get lost. ▶

Follow this path across the complex junction by the Premier Inn hotel and along Barry Island link road opposite and then turn right along Heol Finch. Turn right after passing under the railway and Harbour Road and follow the path along the coast before turning left along The Parade. Once around the bend and heading away from the coast, this road becomes Lakeside and then Romilly Park Road. Follow it around to the right where there is a fine bistro, ride under the railway bridge and uphill

Before World War I Barry Docks were the busiest coal port in the world employing about 8000 women and 10,000 men.

Map continues on page 45

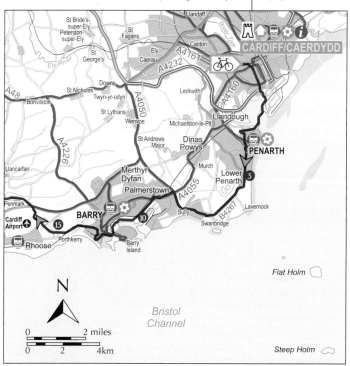

around the perimeter of Romilly Park. Turn left along Park Road and follow it through to **Porthkerry Country Park** where there is a popular café and the first waymarker sign for NCN 88 for many miles. Continue along the shared-use path behind the café and ride under the railway viaduct to join a narrow lane that ends at a junction where a group of attractive thatched cottages sit uncomfortably opposite the perimeter fence of **Cardiff Airport**.

Turn right following a waymarker sign for NCN 88 towards Llantwit Major and ride around the perimeter of the airport. Turn right again near the cargo terminal and follow a shared-use path across the A4226, through **Penmark** (16/51 miles), then **Llanmaes** (22/45 miles) and down to **Llantwit Major** (24/43 miles).

> **Llantwit Major** grew up around Cor Tewdws, a monastery and seminary with over 2000 students, including seven sons of English princes. It is believed to have been founded sometime around AD395, making it the oldest school in Great Britain. It was destroyed by Vikings in AD987 and then closed in 1539 during the Dissolution of the Monasteries. The remains of the monastery are hidden somewhere below St Illtyd's Church in the middle of the village.
>
> Despite rapid growth to accommodate personnel from the local RAF base during the 20th century, the town retains much of its medieval character, making it a desirable place to live for those working in Cardiff and Bridgend, particularly since the railway station reopened in 2005.

Map continues
on page 46

The American tycoon William Randolph Hearst purchased the medieval St Donat's Castle, now the Atlantic College, in 1925 and visited annually until 1936, typically with an entourage of film stars and famous politicians.

Follow NCN 88 down Burial Lane alongside the 15th-century town hall and out into the countryside. Ride through **St Donat's** (25/42 miles) to **Marcross** (26/41 miles). ◄ Although the route runs close to the coast it seldom feels like it. If you want to get closer, or perhaps just stop for a break at the clifftop café, turn left down the lane by the inn in Marcross and ride for 1 mile down to Nash Point where the twin towers of the 19th-century, Grade II listed Nash Lighthouse used to provide a clear

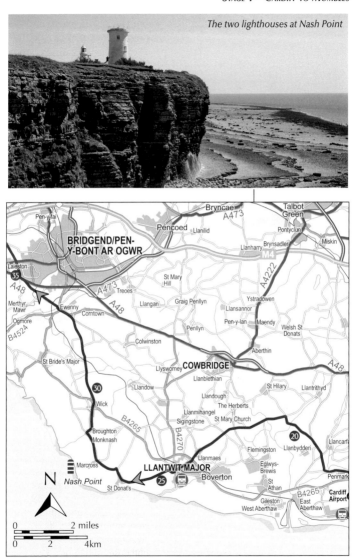

The two lighthouses at Nash Point

45

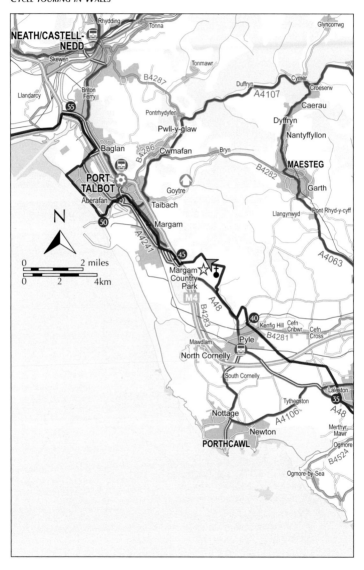

set of 'leading lights' to guide vessels around the dangerous sandbar below the ever-crumbling limestone cliffs.

Return to the main road and ride through **Monknash** (27/40 miles), **Broughton** (28/39 miles) and **Wick** (29/38 miles) to **Ewenny** (32/35 miles) where NCN 88 currently peters out. ▶ Turn right towards Bridgend in the centre of the village and then after 150 metres, turn left along New Inn Road. After 1½ miles, turn left along the **A48** for 300 metres (perhaps resorting to the pavement if the road is busy) and then turn right at the unsigned crossroads and follow this lane across the A473 and along an unnamed lane with a weight restriction. At its end, turn left and quickly left again at a staggered crossroads. Follow this narrow lane for just over a mile going straight across the first junction before turning right at a junction around a triangular patch of grass. Ride downhill passing under the **M4** and over the railway to Pyle (38/29 miles).

Cross into Croft Coch Road at the traffic lights and pass under the railway. Turn right at its end and follow waymarkers for NCN 4 around in a loop to meet the **A48**. Turn right and follow the shared-use path for 1 mile, then turn right towards Margam Discovery Centre. Follow NCN 4 around the perimeter of **Margam Country Park** (41/26 miles), negotiating a pair of narrow iron gates where you may need to remove any panniers to squeeze through. ▶ After you emerge from the country park, turn right in Margam Village, follow the shared-use path across the M4 motorway and then the A48 and continue through **Margam** (45/22 miles) to **Port Talbot** (48/19 miles).

The name **Port Talbot** was first given to the docks in honour of Christopher Rice Mansel Talbot of Margam Castle, who sponsored their development in the 1830s. Eventually, the name was applied to the conurbation formed when the villages of Baglan, Margam and Aberafan merged into each other. Steel-making started in Port Talbot in the first decade of the 20th century, but the town did not become synonymous with steel until the Abbey Works opened in the 1950s. It soon became the

In the first half of the 20th century the three-storeyed maltings in Broughton was run as a welfare hotel, providing low-cost holiday accommodation for miners' families from nearby coalfields.

The 850-acre country park contains the remains of an abbey, a Cistercian monastery and Margam Castle; there is also a neo-Gothic house built by local industrialist Christopher Rice Mansel Talbot (1803–1890).

Map continues on page 49

47

largest steel producer in Europe, employing a labour force of 18,000. Today there are just 4000 employees at the site and like many steel production facilities in the UK and Europe, it has an uncertain future.

Follow NCN 4 signs left across the railway on Oakwood Road, then turn immediately right up Cramic Way joining a path that leads under a flyover across the A4241 and along Riverside Road, with the River Afan to the right and the docks to the left. Cross the footbridge and follow the shared-use path around the roundabout into Afan Way. ◄ Follow waymarkers for NCN 4 across the carriageway and over the blue footbridge into Victoria Road. Turn left into Newbridge Road at the traffic lights and follow this road around to join a shared-use path that runs along the front at **Aberafan** (51/16 miles). After 2 miles follow signs for NCN 4 back inland and ride along Purcell Avenue, Handel Avenue and Seaway Parade to join a shared-use path alongside the A4241 by Baglan Energy Park. Continue along the shared-use path over the M4 and railway and left alongside the A48. Other than for 200 metres in the Swansea suburbs, the final 13 miles of this stage are entirely traffic free.

If you need to make up lost time, continue along the shared-use path that runs alongside Afan Way to rejoin the route at Baglan Energy Park.

SWANSEA

In its heyday Swansea was a major centre for copper, earning it the nickname Copperopolis. The combination of local coal and easy sea access to the copper mines in Devon and Cornwall made Swansea the ideal location for smelting, and during the 18th and 19th centuries the city boomed, and 60% of all the copper ores imported into Great Britain were smelted locally. Although George Borrow wrote that the town had 'some remarkable edifices, spacious and convenient quays, and a commodious harbour', he also said it was 'large, bustling, dirty and gloomy'.

Today the heavy industry has largely gone and the economy of the city relies on the service sector, such as education, health, finance services and public administration. The UK's Driver and Vehicle Licensing Agency is one of the biggest employers locally.

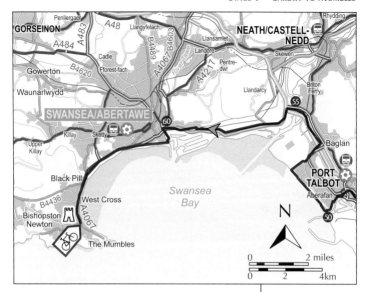

Cross the roundabout, railway and River Neath on the outskirts of **Briton Ferry** (54/13 miles) and then follow NCN 4 under the M4, over the A483 and alongside Fabian Way, past mammoth distribution warehouses, to **Swansea** (60/7 miles), where the shared-use path swings right behind the park and ride car park.

After riding alongside the Fabian Way for 1½ miles, turn left along the eastern bank of the River Tawe, following signs for NCN 4 towards Mumbles. Cross Sail Bridge and ride around Swansea Bay to **Black Pill** (65/2 miles). At weekends this stretch of path is very popular with recreational cyclists, joggers and dog-walkers, so progress may be slow. If you are going straight on to Stage 2, turn right at the aptly named Junction Café and follow NCN 4 towards Llanelli. But if you are heading into Mumbles for an overnight stay or simply a break, continue along the shared-use path around the bay for the final 2 miles of this stage.

Looking across Swansea Bay from above Mumbles Pier

Mumbles marks the start of the wonderful Gower Peninsula. For the sake of brevity, it is left out of this tour. However, you could stay over in Mumbles for an extra night and enjoy a day without panniers, visiting some of its famous beaches. Mumbles itself is a vibrant seaside village with plenty of shops, restaurants and pubs that attract day-trippers from all over the region. Food fans should try the local oysters. But if you are not so keen on seafood, you will be spoilt for choice when it comes to ice cream parlours.

Adding in a loop around the Gower Peninsula

The 27-mile loop around the Gower Peninsula starts at Mumbles and rejoins the circular route at Gowerton, adding 20 miles to the circumnavigation. Start at the mini roundabout on the front below Oystermouth Castle and cycle inland along Newton Road towards Caswell. After two-thirds of mile, turn left into Newton Road. Ride up the short hill, turn left at the top and then turn immediately right into Nottage Road and drop down to join Caswell Road.

Turn right by the church and ride around Caswell Bay (2/25 miles) and into Bishopton (3/24 miles). Turn left along Pyle Road and then after another mile turn left along the B4426 towards Port Eynon. Ride through Kittle to Pennard (6/21 miles) and then turn right into Linkside Drive and follow it to the junction with the B4118 in the centre of Parkmill (5/22 miles). Turn left and ride through Penmaen (7/20 miles) and Nicholaston (8/24 miles) and then turn left by the gatehouse of Penrice Castle. Ride through Oxwich (10/17 miles), then turn left towards Horton.

If you are staying overnight at the hostel in Port Eynon, turn left when you meet the A4118. Otherwise turn right, ride through Scurlage (15/12 miles) and then turn left towards Burry Green. Turn right towards Llanrhidian in Burry Green (18/9 miles) and ride through Oldwalls to Llanrhidian (21/6 miles). Turn left into the village, follow this quiet lane along the coast to Crofty (23/4 miles) and then turn left along the B4295 and ride through Penclawdd (25/2 miles). Join the shared-use path as you approach Gowerton and turn left at the traffic lights on Pont-y-Cob Road to rejoin the route, following waymarker signs for NCN 4.

RIDING ANTICLOCKWISE

If this is your last day and you think you might miss the train you are due to catch in Cardiff, remember you can curtail your ride early and catch a train into Cardiff at one of the many stations along this stage.

STAGE 2
Mumbles to Tenby

Start	Below Oystermouth Castle, Mumbles (SS 616 885)
Finish	Tenby Railway Station (SN 129 006)
Distance	73 miles (117km)
Ascent	1300m
Time	10–11hr
OS maps	OS Landranger 159 and 158
Refreshments	There are cafés, pubs and shops just off route all along this stage, but little on it other than at Kidwelly, Ferryside, Carmarthen, Laugharne, Amroth, Saundersfoot and Tenby
Accommodation	Plenty of B&Bs and hotels in the towns and coastal resorts but the only hostels are in Llansteffan and Manorbier, which is 5 miles beyond Tenby just off route on Stage 3.

After the first 2 miles, Stage 2 follows NCN 4 all the way to Tenby, making route-finding remarkably easy. The first 30 miles are fairly flat so ground is covered quickly. But once beyond Kidwelly the route becomes much more undulating until the final few miles around Carmarthen Bay.

People from Gowerton are locally referred to as 'starch', as it was traditionally the village where white collar workers employed in heavy industry in Swansea chose to live.

Ride back north on the shared-use path around Swansea Bay as far as Black Pill, retracing the final two miles of Stage 1. Turn left and follow NCN 4 away from the coast on a shared-use path that follows the track, once used by the Heart of Wales railway, up through the Clyne Valley Country Park, passing close to **Dunvant** (5/68miles) and **Gowerton** (7/66 miles). ◄ Follow the waymarker signs through the residential estate and out of the village alongside the B4295, then turn right into Ponty Cob Road. After a mile pass under the railway and the **A484** and then turn immediately left along a shared-use path to the south of Loughor (8/65 miles).

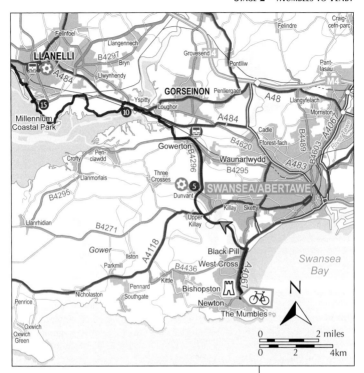

After a mile, cross the River Loughor and turn right following waymarker signs for NCN 4 around Yspitty (9/64 miles). Cross the main road at the end of the village

Map continues on page 54

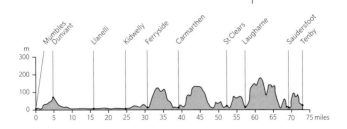

A trail-side plaque near Pwll commemorates the place where a seaplane carrying Amelia Earhart landed in 1928, making her the first woman to fly across the Atlantic. She made a solo crossing four years later.

and ride around the perimeter of the car park and across the footbridge over the A484. Ride along this meandering and generously wide shared-use path through the **Millennium Coastal Park**, first passing the holiday park, then swinging inland around the Wildfowl and Wetlands Centre before returning to the coast by a smart development of New-England-style homes on the outskirts of Llanelli.

Continue following NCN 4 alongside the B4304, then turn left at the next roundabout by Llanelli Dock and ride out along the coast and enjoy mile after mile of traffic-free cycling past Pwll to **Burry Port** (20/53 miles). ◄ Ride around the harbour at Burry Port, which

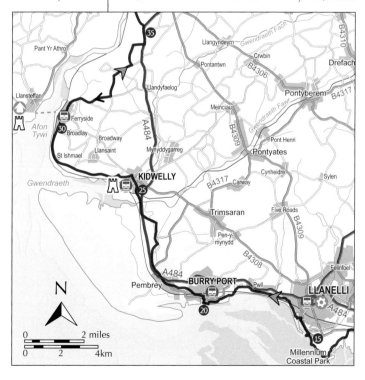

54

Passing an iconic Welsh signpost in the Millennium Coastal Park near Burry Port

was established to ship coal from mines further up the Gwendraeth Valley, and follow NCN 4 inland through **Pembrey** (21/52 miles) and **Kidwelly** (25/48 miles). Turn left immediately after the bridge over Gwendraeth Fach in the centre of the village and ride back out to the coast at the mouth of the River Towy.

Map continues on page 56

KIDWELLY CASTLE

The Normans established the first motte and bailey castle at Kidwelly in 1106, but Edward I commissioned a stone castle with two sets of concentric walls in the 13th century as part of his 'Ring of Steel' fortresses that were introduced to control the Welsh. However, it was only completed in 1422 due to local uprisings in support of the Welsh rebel, Owain Glyndŵr, who was trying to regain Wales's independence from the English crown.

Unlike many Welsh castles, Kidwelly survived the ravages of the English Civil War and is remarkably well preserved. It was used as a location during the filming of *Monty Python and the Holy Grail*. To visit the castle, continue around the bend and turn immediately right into Castle Street by the coffee shop.

If you can, ride out of Llansteffan following signs first to Llanybri and from there signs to St Clears to rejoin NCN 4.

When you reach **Ferryside** (30/43 miles), you may be able to take the recently reintroduced ferry service across the river to Llansteffan, saving 18 miles. ◀ Otherwise follow NCN 4 through the village and uphill to briefly join the A484 and then turn left and ride through **Croesyceiliog** and down into **Carmarthen** (39/34 miles). Turn left along the shared-use path alongside the A484, which leads into the town, and follow it across the A48, under the A40 and down Pensarn Road towards the River Towy. Turn left immediately before the bridge and follow NCN 4 around past Carmarthen Station.

Map continues on page 59

Cross the footbridge over the River Towy, loop back underneath it and follow a shared-use path along the

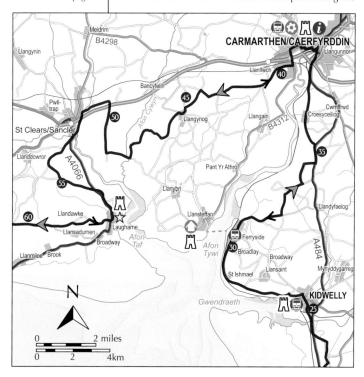

56

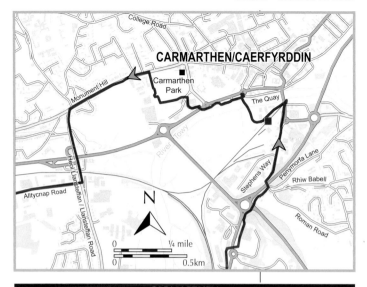

CARMARTHEN

The Greco-Roman polymath Ptolemy mentioned Carmarthen in his writings, providing the town with convincing evidence to support its claim that it is the oldest in Wales. Between the 16th and 18th centuries it was certainly the most populous borough in Wales, but was soon outgrown by towns in the South Wales Coalfield during the 19th century.

Carmarthen Castle, which dates from the 12th century, was captured and destroyed on several occasions, and Oliver Cromwell ordered it to be dismantled in the mid 1600s. However, it remained remarkably intact and housed the town's police station during the Victorian era, the local gaol until the 1920s and is still home to a small museum and the town's Tourist Information Centre.

riverbank and through Carmarthen Park. Turn left along the B4312 and left again into **Llansteffan Road** half a mile further on. Once over the A40 and the railway, turn right into **Alltycnap Road** and follow NCN 4 as it snakes uphill. Near the top of the climb, turn right and immediately right again, all the time following signs for NCN 4. Follow this pleasant, narrow lane enjoying the views of the rolling hills to the north before descending to cross **Afon Cywyn**.

Turn left when you meet the A40 and follow the shared-use path towards **St Clears** (52/21 miles). As you approach the village, turn sharply left and drop down to join a shared-use path alongside Afon Cynin. Turn left

LAUGHARNE

Laugharne is a pretty town with pleasant Georgian townhouses and the ruins of a 12th-century castle that the Parliamentarians besieged and dismantled in 1642. Had Margaret Taylor, the first wife of the noted historian AJP Taylor, not purchased the Boathouse in Laugharne for the Welsh poet and writer Dylan Thomas (1914–1953), who had

The Boathouse at Laugharne where the poet Dylan Thomas lived for the last four years of his short life

once been her lover, it would have probably remained a sleepy backwater. Thomas clearly loved the place, and it is thought to have inspired the fictional town of Llareggub in his most enduring work, *Under Milk Wood*. However, other places that have a fleeting association with Thomas further along our route make similar claims.

Thomas and his family stayed for just four years until his early death in 1953, which was brought about by a notoriously excessive lifestyle. Thomas is buried in the town's churchyard and despite a stormy marriage beset by drunkenness and infidelity, his wife Caitlin (1913–1994), who left Laugharne at the earliest opportunity, chose to be buried next to him. Today, the place that Thomas called a 'timeless, mild, beguiling island of a town' celebrates him and other Welsh culture in an annual literary and arts festival called the Laugharne Weekend, which takes place in April. See www.thelaugharneweekend.com for further details.

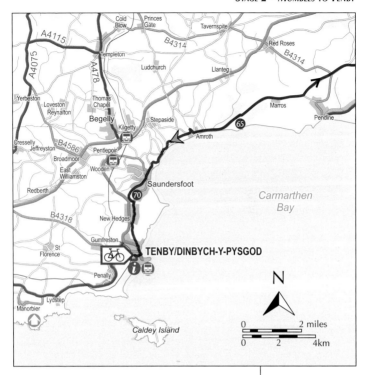

at its end and ride along Bridge Street. Then turn right towards New Mill just after crossing the bridge over **Afon Taf**. A mile further on, turn left and follow NCN 4 way-markers towards Laugharne and enjoy 2 miles of descent before turning right along the A4066 to **Laugharne** (57/16 miles). ▸

When you are ready to leave, turn into The Grist, a triangular space in the centre of the village surrounded on all sides by pubs and shops. Climb steadily for 4 miles, first in deep shade between banks of ferns then between neatly tended hedgerows. Near the top there are wonderful views out across Carmarthen Bay and back along the coast towards the Gower Peninsula. Cross the

If you want to bypass Laugharne, continue through New Mill, saving 4 miles and 160m of ascent.

TENBY

Gaily painted houses around the harbour at Tenby

Its sheltered position in Carmarthen Bay on the far west coast of Britain made Tenby an obvious location for a fortified settlement. The Normans built the original castle out on the rocky promontory in the 12th century. Over the following centuries various rulers extended the castle, building new curtain walls, towers and gates to enclose a large part of the settlement known today as the 'old town'. However, its defences did little to stop the Royalists and then the Parliamentarians ravaging the town in 1648.

Soon afterwards, an outbreak of the plague killed half the population and the town fell into a decline that lasted for over a century. The cleric John Wesley (1703–1791) noted that 'two-thirds of the old town is in ruins or has entirely vanished. Pigs roam among the abandoned houses and Tenby presents a dismal spectacle'. Its fortunes were only reversed during the Napoleonic Wars, which prevented the British aristocracy from making Grand Tours across Europe. Spotting an opportunity, Sir William Paxton (1744–1824), a Scottish-born sailor who had made his fortune in the East India Company before settling locally, set about transforming the town into a fashionable resort. He built spa baths and hotels and established a string of coaching inns to bring visitors from Swansea. His initiative succeeded and Tenby continued to flourish even when travel within Europe resumed following the victory at the Battle of Trafalgar in 1815.

The old town castle walls and the majority of the Georgian and colourful Victorian buildings have survived. As a result there are over 370 listed buildings and other structures in and around Tenby, making it a very attractive place to visit no matter how long your stay.

B4314 and enjoy one mile of rapid descent. Turn right at the bottom of the hill, ride past the inn and climb up through **Marros** (64/9 miles) before dropping down to the coast by Amroth Castle. Enjoy the views of Tenby and Saundersfoot across Carmarthen Bay on the descent and at the bottom look out for the New Inn, which has a track pump for cyclists to use. It also carries a small selection of essentials, such as inner tubes and energy bars.

Climb the hill out of **Amroth** (67/6 miles) and turn left near the top on to the Pembrokeshire Coast Path, which has a good tarmac surface and gives superb views out across the bay. Descend to Wiseman's Bridge, where the route briefly rejoins the road before following a shared-used path around the coast and through two short tunnels through the cliffs to **Saundersfoot** (69/5 miles).

Ride through this bustling seaside resort and turn right up Stammers Road, following waymarkers for NCN 4. Near the top of the hill, pick up a shared-use path that runs alongside the A478 and follow it around into Old Narberth Road. Ride down past the town cemetery along a stretch of superbly smooth road, which guarantees locals a comfortable final journey, and then turn left into Tenby where the stage ends.

RIDING ANTICLOCKWISE

If you are planning to take the recently reintroduced ferry service across the Towy Estuary between Llansteffan and Ferryside, avoid disappointment by first checking that it is running before you leave NCN 4 and head down to Llansteffan (see www. carmarthenbayferries.com).

STAGE 3
Tenby to Fishguard

Start	Tenby Railway Station (SN 129 006)
Finish	Fishguard & Goodwick Railway Station (SM 945 382)
Distance	64 miles (102km)
Ascent	1200m
Time	9–10hr
OS maps	OS Landranger 158 and 157
Refreshments	Generally lots of choice apart from the final 15 miles beyond St David's, where there is only a handful of cafés and pubs and some may even be closed out of season
Accommodation	Plenty of accommodation of all types around the coast, including hostels at Broad Haven, St David's, Trefin and Trefasser, just off route near Fishguard

This stage follows NCN 4, making route-finding easy. The first half of the stage is fairly flat and progress can be quite fast, However, after Board Haven the riding becomes more demanding due to the almost constant undulations along the quiet lanes around the coast. But there are plenty of attractions to visit for those on a more leisurely schedule, including Pembroke Castle and St David's Cathedral.

In St Florence look out for the massive Flemish chimneys, a style thought to have originated with the immigrants encouraged to settle in the area by Henry I and Henry II during the 12th century to help develop the local wool trade.

Ride south along Station Road, heading away from the town, then turn right, cross the railway and follow NCN 4 through the holiday park and across the A4139 before turning right into Trefyloyne Lane. Ride through **St Florence** (4/60 miles) and then turn left at a junction where the blue waymarker plate for NCN 4 is the only road sign. ◀

After a mile, turn left and then half a mile further on turn right towards Pembroke. Easy riding along a broad ridge gives an occasional view of Carew Castle 2 miles to the north and the oil refineries at Milford Haven to the west. Follow NCN 4 through **Lamphey** (9/55 miles) and

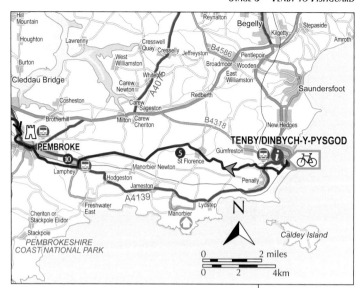

then turn right along Lower Lamphey Road immediately after crossing the railway and ride into **Pembroke** (11/53 miles). Turn right on to a shared-use path that leads around into Main Street and follow waymarkers for NCN 4 left into Goose's Lane. Cross the town's inner ring road and follow the path through Lower Common Park, across Bridgend Terrace and out along the river with Pembroke Castle standing high above the opposite bank.

Cross the river and follow waymarkers for NCN 4 up Castle View before turning left on to a shared-use path

Map continues on page 65

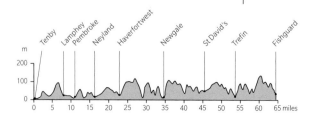

PEMBROKE CASTLE

Most of what remains of Pembroke Castle was built by William Marshal (1146/7–1219), who was reputed to be 'the best knight that ever lived'. During the 12th century he diligently served five kings: Henry II, Henry the Young King (who was crowned during his father's lifetime), Richard I, John and Henry III. All of Marshal's sons

Pembroke Castle seen from the shared-use path on the opposite bank of Pembroke River

died childless, so the castle passed back to the crown and was subsequently granted to a number of the king's favourites. After the English War Oliver Cromwell ordered the castle to be destroyed and encouraged townspeople to reuse its stone for their own purposes. The castle was then allowed to decay, with little done to conserve its structure.

It was rescued by Major General Sir Ivor Philipps, MP, (1861–1940), who purchased the castle in 1928 and set about restoring its walls, gate-houses and towers. After his death a trust was set up for the castle, jointly managed by his descendants and the town council. The castle is open to the public and is the largest privately owned castle in Wales.

alongside the A4319. Follow this path uphill and left along Pembroke Road. After half a mile, just before the houses begin, turn right and follow a shared-use path down the hill to **Pembroke Dock** (13/51 miles).

Pembroke Dock was founded as a naval dockyard in 1814, subsequently attracting both the army and the air force, making it an important garrison town. Most of the military have left leaving high unemployment and numerous empty buildings, including a hangar where Han Solo's iconic craft, the Millennium Falcon, from *Star Wars*, was constructed in 1979.

Map continues
on page 67

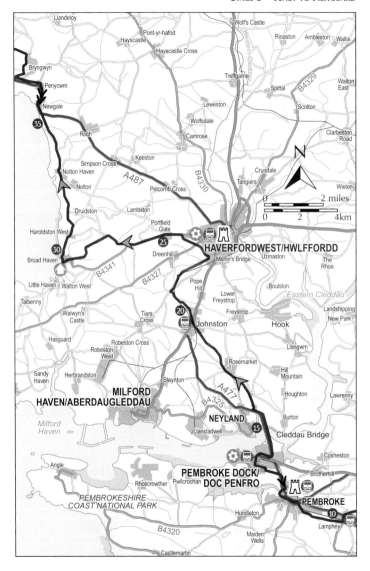

When the path ends, continue along Gwyther Street and turn right along the wonderfully broad Meyrick Street. Cross at the next junction to join another stretch of shared-use path that runs alongside Western Way and London Road before swinging left along Waterloo Road to follow the old road alongside the **A477**.

Cross **Cleddau Bridge** (15/49 miles), which opened in 1975 replacing a steam ferry that ran between Pembroke Dock and Neyland, then half a mile further on cross a much shorter bridge across Westfield Pill, which provides a safe haven for Neyland Marina. Cross the main road and drop down to join a path that follows the track of an old railway line which runs northwards for 6 miles through **Johnston** (20/44 miles) to the outskirts of Haverfordwest (23/41 miles). This branch line opened in 1856 linking Neyland, which was an important port for Ireland until the new harbour opened at Fishguard in 1906, into the national rail network. The line closed in 1964 leaving a wonderful green corridor that is popular with local walkers and cyclists.

Unless you want to visit Haverfordwest, which is a mile off route, turn left and follow waymarker signs for NCN 4 along Bethany Road and Palmerston Road, across the B4327 and into Park Corner Road, which runs alongside Haverfordwest race course. At its end, turn left towards Broad Haven following a shared-use path along the B4341. Ride through **Portfield Gate** (25/39 miles). After a mile, turn right towards Nolton and then left into Long Lane a mile further on and descend to **Broad Haven** (29/35 miles), which has an ample selection of places to eat.

When you are ready to leave Broad Haven, rejoin NCN 4 near the seafront and ride up Haroldstone Hill. Turn left after 1 mile and ride through Druidston Haven (32/31 miles) and **Nolton Haven** (33/30 miles) to join the A487 at **Newgale** (35/29 miles) where there is a glorious three-mile stretch of beach that is popular with surfers and windsurfers. The ridge of low hills that run inland from Newgale mark the boundary between English-speaking and Welsh-speaking Pembrokeshire,

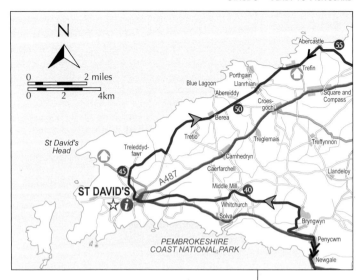

with English place names to the south and Welsh place names to the north.

Map continues on page 69

LITTLE ENGLAND BEYOND WALES

Despite being in remote West Wales, the inhabitants of Pembrokeshire and Carmarthenshire are more likely to speak English than their immediate neighbours, and the region is sometimes referred to as 'Little England beyond Wales'. When historians started to study this linguistic division in the early 20th century, they used the Anglo Saxon word *landsker* (visible boundary) to describe the phenomenon that is reflected in local place names.

The area within the Landsker Line includes 50 castles and strongholds built and garrisoned by the Normans and Flemish soldiers in the 11th and 12th centuries to protect the communities from their homelands who settled there. Evidence of this settlement persists, and a genetic study in 2005 revealed marked differences in the DNA profiles of inhabitants on opposite sides of the Landsker Line, with the 2011 census finding a far smaller proportion of Welsh speakers in the area to its south.

Climb steeply out of Newgale, ride through **Penycwn** and then turn right towards Brawdy Business Park. After 500 metres, turn left and left again by a caravan park a mile further on. Follow this quiet lane down to Middle Mill (40/24 miles), cross the River Solva and ride through **Whitchurch** to St David's (44/20 miles). Join the A487 and ride into the city.

Because of its cathedral, **St David's** was granted city status by Queen Elizabeth II in 1994, although in reality it is little bigger than a large village. Saint David (c. 500–c. 589), the patron saint of Wales, who is buried in the cathedral, established a monastic community there, although the present cathedral dates from the 12th century, with subsequent bishops adding to its structure.

Cromwell's forces did their best to destroy the cathedral, and it was not restored until years later when the regency architect John Nash (1752–1835) and the Gothic revivalist architect George Gilbert Scott (1811–1878) were commissioned on various restoration projects.

St David, the patron saint of Wales, is buried in the 12th-century St David's Cathedral

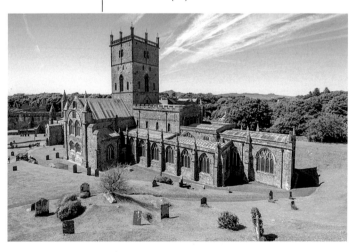

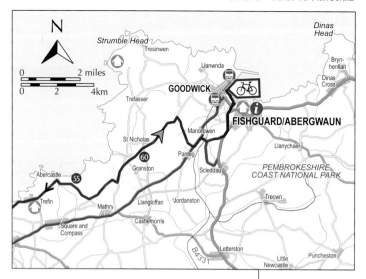

Turn right towards Fishguard at the Market Cross and then immediately left into The Peebles and ride past St David's Cathedral and out into the countryside. For the next 20 miles, until this stage ends in Fishguard, the route sticks as close to the coast as possible. However, you rarely feel close to the sea unless you drop down to one of the pretty coastal villages, such as Abereiddy or Porthgain, both of which appear on road signs and are less than a mile off route. ▶ Ride on through **Llanrhian** (51/13 miles) and Trefin (53/11 miles), where the Mill Café sells inner tubes and other essentials, and **Abercastle** (54/10 miles), where the sea remains elusively out of sight just down the hill.

After 4 miles of easy route-finding, turn right and drop down Manorowen Hill, then turn left along the A487 and then after 600 metres turn right towards Haverfordwest. Turn left immediately after crossing the railway and a mile later join a shared-use path alongside the A40. Turn right after half a mile and follow signs for NCN 82 and 47 if you are heading into Fishguard or

In recent years the Red Bull Cliff Diving World Series has visited the Blue Lagoon, a flooded slate quarry a mile off route on the coast near Abereiddy.

continuing directly on to Stage 4. Otherwise continue to the coast and then turn left along the front to Fishguard & Goodwick Railway Station where this stage ends.

RIDING ANTICLOCKWISE

If hostels are your preferred accommodation, try the one at Manorbier, just off route, four miles before Tenby.

FISHGUARD

Fishguard is divided into two parts: the main town of Fishguard and Lower Town on the coast at the bottom of Hill Terrace, which is believed to be the site of the original fishing village. The Royal Oak in the main town is where a force of 1400 French soldiers, who had landed near Fishguard two days earlier, finally surrendered in 1797, giving the town the notoriety of being the location of the last invasion of Britain. The failed invasion made a heroine of local girl Jemima Nicholas (1750–1832), who rounded up 12 drunken French soldiers with a pitchfork and forced them to surrender.

Once a busy herring port, Lower Town was used as the setting for Llareggub in the 1972 film of Dylan Thomas's *Under Milk Wood*, which starred Richard Burton, Elizabeth Taylor and Peter O'Toole.

The harbour at Lower Fishguard was used as Llareggub in the 1972 film of Dylan Thomas's Under Milk Wood

STAGE 4
Fishguard to Aberaeron

Start	Fishguard & Goodwick Railway Station (SM 945 382)
Finish	Market Street, Aberaeron (SN 456 629)
Distance	55 miles (88km)
Ascent	1500m
Time	9–10hr
OS maps	OS Landranger 157, 145,146 and 135
Refreshments	Lots of choice in the many resorts and towns along the route
Accommodation	Plenty of B&Bs and guest houses along the coast, but the only hostels are at Newport, Cardigan and Poppit Sands in the early part of the stage

This stage follows NCN 82 for the first 24 miles to Cardigan, which makes route-finding easy. But after this stage more detailed directions are provided, as the route follows minor roads between the pretty villages along the coast. Most of these are old fishing villages where freshwater rivers run down to the sea. This provides a fair amount of climbing between one valley and the next. However, the hills are short, rarely steep and there is plenty of time to recover in between them.

From the start at Fishguard & Goodwick Railway Station, ride along the shared-use path along the promenade and follow waymarker signs for NCN 82 towards **Fishguard**

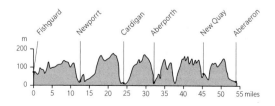

(2/53 miles). Ride through the town, follow waymarkers for NCN 82 into Hamilton Street and climb steadily
up the delightful wooded valley of Cwm Gwaun. Ride
through the little villages of Llanychaer (3/52 miles),
Pontfaen (6/49 miles) and Cilgwyn (10/45 miles) and then

NEWPORT

In medieval times Newport was a busy port, shipping out wool and pottery
some of which was probably fired in a 15th-century kiln that is believed
to be the only intact example in Britain. The old port area, which is down
on the Parrog estuary, remains well preserved with old quay walls and two
former lime kilns. Today, the port provides moorings for small craft, and
the nearby cottages are mostly holiday lets. With care it is possible to wade
across the River Parrog at low tide and visit the sandy beach on the opposite
shore, which is a 3½-mile journey by road.

During the summers of the 1880s, the landscape painter, John Brett
(1831–1902), a lesser-known member of the Pre-Raphaelite movement,
rented Newport Castle, which had been restored as a dwelling in the middle
of the century, and moored his 210-ton schooner, *Viking*, at Parrog. In his
boat he travelled the length of the Pembroke coast painting coastal scenes
and seascapes that are now highly sought after.

Looking towards Newport Boat Club on the Parrog estuary

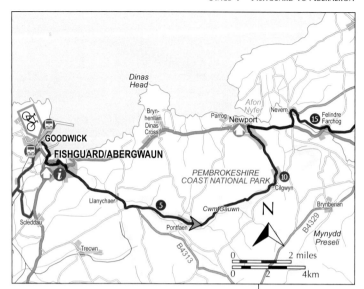

follow the NCN 82 back down to the coast at Newport (13/42 miles). ▶

Unless you want to explore this pretty town, turn right following NCN 82 towards Cardigan. Turn left after 1½ miles and cycle around a loop around **Nevern** (15/40miles). The classically braided Nevern Cross in the village churchyard dates from the 10th or 11th century. The nearby Vitalianus Stone dates from around AD500 and is inscribed in Latin. After passing through the centre of the village, turn right along a bridleway that runs alongside Afon Nyfer to rejoin the A487 in **Felindre Farchog** (17/38 miles). After rain this track can be muddy, and those with skinny tyres are advised to ignore this loop around Nevern and continue along the A487 to Felindre Farchog.

After 400 metres turn left into a narrow lane, climb past Castell Henllys, an Iron Age hill fort reconstructed on its original foundations, and rejoin the A487 again 2½ miles further on. Turn left, ride through **Llantood**

The Dyffryn Arms in Pontfaen has been run by the same family since 1840 and remains a much-loved retreat for those who enjoy simple pleasures and beer straight from the barrel.

Map continues on page 75

Looking across Afon Teifi to Cardigan Castle

(20/35 miles) and then turn left towards Moylgrove. Turn right, ride across the next junction and then turn sharp right near the top of the hill and descend steeply into **St Dogmaels** (24/31 miles). Turn right and follow the road along the bank of Afon Teifi into **Cardigan** (25/30 miles) where the route stops following NCN 82.

CARDIGAN

Cardigan grew up around the Norman castle, which was built in the late 11th or early 12th century. By the 18th century it had become an important port for both merchant boats and herring fishing. However, its shallow harbour could not accommodate modern boats, so by the early 20th century shipping had more or less ceased. Today, the town is the commercial centre for the vast agricultural hinterland beyond it.

Ceredigion County Council purchased Cardigan Castle from its last private owner in 2003 and undertook a 10-year-long programme of fundraising, repair and regeneration. This included creating a heritage centre, building an all-day restaurant and restoring Castle Green House, a Georgian mansion within the castle walls that now offers B&B and self-catering accommodation. See www.cardigancastle.com for details.

Turn left, cross the river and cycle up High Street. Turn left towards Theatr Mwldan and follow Bath House Road away from the town. Turn left along the B4548 towards Gwbert, then turn right towards Mwnt, a quarter of a mile further on. At the end of this lane turn right, ride along the ridge through **Felinwynt** (31/24 miles) and then turn left towards **Aberporth** (33/22 miles). Cruise down into the village past the missile range. ▶

Turn left and cycle along the front and through the upper part of the village. Turn right at the mini roundabout by the Y Morlan Inn and 300 metres later turn left along FFordd Tresaith. Ride through Tresaith (35/20 miles) and then 2 miles further on, just after passing a well-tended

Aberporth was a centre for herring fishing until the early 20th century. Crab and lobster are still fished here today.

Map continues on page 76

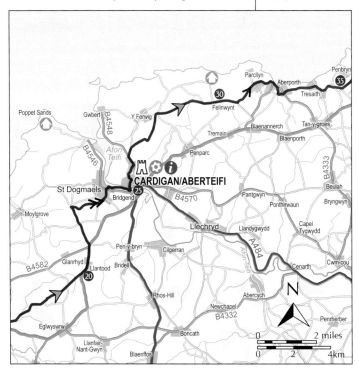

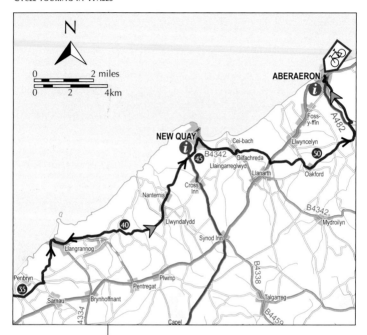

chapel with a prominent monkey puzzle tree, turn left
and drop down to the pretty coastal resort of **Llangrannog**
(39/16 miles), where a statue of the 6th-century abbot St
Carannog, who is credited with founding Llangrannog,
looks down upon the village.

Ride along the front and then turn inland and climb
away from the coast, following the A4321. A mile further
on, just before Pontgarreg, turn left towards Llwyndafydd.
Cycle through **Llwyndafydd** (44/11 miles), and then 2 ½
miles further on cross the A486 and ride down Francis
Road to **New Quay** (46/9 miles).

Turn left along Margaret Street for the town centre. Otherwise turn right and follow the B4342 to
Gilfachreda (48/7 miles). Turn left at the end of the village and follow this meandering lane around to a junction by Wern Chapel. Turn right, cross the A487 a mile

NEW QUAY

New Quay is now a busy resort, but during the 19th century it was an important centre for shipbuilding that had a number of shipwrights, half a dozen blacksmith shops, three sailmakers, three ropewalks and a foundry. After shipbuilding ceased in the 1870s, the town's menfolk often became mariners or found employment in occupations linked with the sea.

You can still see lengths of chain, metal rings and capstans as well as many of the old warehouses, which have since been put to new uses, along the quay. The poet and writer Dylan Thomas briefly lived locally during the winter of 1944–45, and the town is often cited as partial inspiration for his fictitious village of Llareggub in *Under Milk Wood*. You can follow the Dylan Thomas Walking Trail around the town.

further on and then turn immediately left at an unsigned junction. Turn right at the end of this road and then half a mile later turn left in the centre in the pretty and very English-sounding village of **Oakford** (51/4 miles), heading towards Neuaddlwyd. After 2 miles turn left on the A482 towards Aberaeron and then a third of a mile later turn sharply right following a blue marker sign for a cycle route. After 200 metres, turn left and follow the cycle trail that runs alongside Afon Aeron into Aberaeron. ▸

Llanerchaeron, an elegant 18th-century mansion that is said to be the best early work of the architect John Nash, is situated half a mile off route in the Aeron Valley.

ABERAERON

Aberaeron as it is today was planned and developed by the Rev. Alban Thomas Jones Gwynne (1749–1819) during the first two decades of the 19th century. Born locally into a noted family, he followed an elder brother into the church and became a county rector in rural Hampshire. He returned to Wales to marry in 1797 and soon inherited Monachty, a substantial local estate, from a cousin. This brought with it the title of Lord of the Manor of Aberaeron, which was then just a collection of houses and a small quay trapped between the sea and the turnpike road. At his own expense, he excavated the harbour and built new piers. Following his death in 1819, his son, Colonel Alban Gwynne (1784–1861), commissioned the noted Shrewsbury architect John Hiram Haycock to design and develop the new town around the central Alban Square.

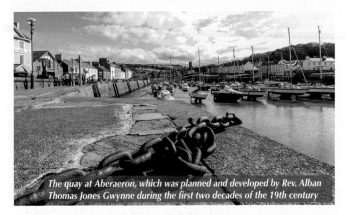

The quay at Aberaeron, which was planned and developed by Rev. Alban Thomas Jones Gwynne during the first two decades of the 19th century

In the following decades Colonel Alban Gwynne added numerous notable buildings, including the town hall and the market hall. During the 19th century Aberaeron became a bustling port and commercial centre with its own woollen mill and an ironworks famous for forging the Aberaeron Shovel, which with a triangular blade and a long curved handle was said to be easier to use than a traditional shovel.

The success of the town's harbour went into decline after 1911 when a branch line was opened between Aberaeron and Lampeter, connecting the town to the wider rail network. However, the railway was never commercially viable and the passenger service was withdrawn in 1951 just after the railways were nationalised. Goods traffic continued until 1973.

In creating an attractive Georgian town with many fine buildings, the Gwynne family left an unexpected legacy in tourism, which is the mainstay of Aberaeron's local economy today. It can justly claim to be the Jewel of Cardigan Bay.

RIDING ANTICLOCKWISE

This is certainly the hardest stage in the circumnavigation, and possibly harder still when riding north to south, so allow plenty of time for breaks.

STAGE 5
Aberaeron to Machynlleth

Start	Market Street, Aberaeron (SN 456 629)
Finish	Machynlleth Railway Station (SH 745 013)
Distance	43 miles (69km)
Ascent	1100m
Time	7–8 hr
OS maps	OS Landranger 135
Refreshments	Plenty of choice at the major centres along the stage
Accommodation	Plenty of accommodation of all types around the coast, including hostels at Llanrhystud, Borth and Machynlleth

To avoid the busier roads along the coast, this stage heads inland to more undulating terrain. However, the hills are never severe and are soon over, and the second half of the stage across the coastal plain around Borth and alongside the Dyfi estuary is far easier. Other than Aberystwyth itself, there are few attractions along the way, making it a day to enjoy the scenery and perhaps a dip in the sea.

Head north out of Aberaeron towards Aberystwyth and follow a shared-use path alongside the A487. After a mile, turn right by a solitary bungalow called Trewylan. Climb steeply up through the tiny hilltop village of Llanddewi Aberarth, which gives spectacular views out across

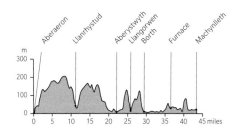

79

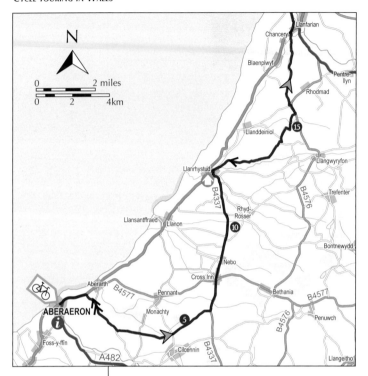

To reach the shingle beach at Llanrhystud, ride through the village along the A487 and turn right into the single track road just south of the petrol station and convenience store.

Map continues on page 83

Cardigan Bay, and then turn right towards Cilcennin. Go straight on at the next crossroads, enjoying the easy cycling, and then turn left along the B4337 towards **Cross Inn**. Follow the B4337 for 5 miles through Cross Inn (7/37 miles) and Nebo to **Llanrhystud** (11/32 miles). ◄

Turn right just before the village, cross the footbridge alongside the ford and then turn right into a narrow road alongside Afon Wyre. After three miles of steady climbing, turn left opposite a pair of galvanized farm gates. Follow this narrow road for 1½ miles and then turn left at its end. After 500 metres turn left towards Llanddeiniol and then immediately right into a narrow road. After 2½ miles turn right along the A487 towards **Llanfarian**

(18/25 miles), perhaps resorting to the footpath if traffic is heavy. After 300 metres bear left at the war memorial and ride around this quiet lane with panoramic views of Aberystwyth to the north. Turn right half a mile further on and continue past Llanchyaearn Church and over Afon Ystwyth. After passing Gosein Chapel, turn left to join NCN 81 and follow it through Trefechan (21/22 miles) and over Afon Rheidol into **Aberystwyth** (22/21 miles). Turn left along the northern bank of the river and ride around to the seafront.

Looking north from the war memorial on the promenade at Aberystwyth

ABERYSTWYTH

Although Aberystwyth gets its name from its position at the mouth of Afon Ystwyth, it is Afon Rheidol that passes through the modern town, which expanded to the north of the original settlement around Pendinas. The arrival of the railway in 1864 triggered a boom in tourism, with the town once advertised as the 'Biarritz of Wales'.

During this time a number of hotels were built to cater for tourists, including the Castle Hotel, which was developed around an older building designed by the regency architect John Nash. However, the developers were bankrupted by a sudden collapse in the Stock Exchange in 1865. The unfinished hotel was acquired for a fraction of the £80,000 the developers had sunk into the project by the Welsh National University Committee, a group of people seeking to establish a Welsh university that could award degrees for a range of subjects. They achieved their goal and the University College of Wales (later becoming Aberystwyth University) was founded in 1872 with an initial intake of 26 students. Today, the University, which has almost 10,000 students, has largely relocated to campuses away from the coast and Old College is set to be given a new lease of life as an exhibition centre and a hub for creative business start-ups.

The students and staff of the university now outnumber the town's population; so too do the tens of thousands of starlings that perform extraordinary displays of synchronised aerobatics on autumn evenings before roosting on Aberystwyth Pier.

Ride past Aberystwyth Castle, the Old College and the town's famous pier and then turn right into Albert Street. Ride past the now disused Ceredigion County

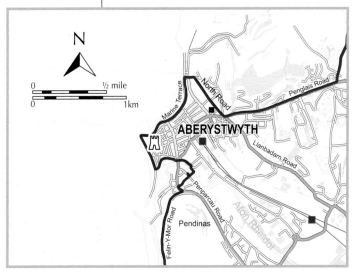

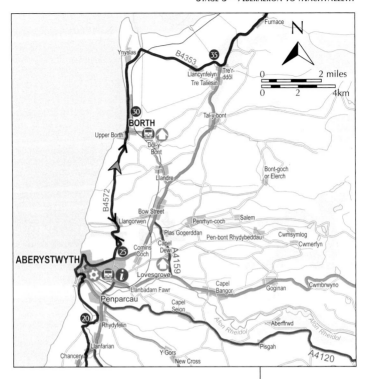

Hall, cross the next junction and follow North Road to its end. ▶ Turn left along **Penglais Road**, making use of the shared-use path, ride past the university campus and then turn left towards Llangorwen.

Ride uphill away from the city before dropping steeply down to cross Afon Clarach. Continue through **Llangorwen** (26/17 miles) and then climb through a range of low hills that obscures the sea until the steep descent into **Borth** (30/13 miles). The shallow waters and three-mile expanse of golden sand make Borth a popular resort, particularly for surfing and kite surfing. Ride through Borth and out across the flatlands around **Llancynfelyn**, which in the absence of a headwind are

Fans of the Welsh detective drama 'Hinterland' may recognize Ceredigion County Hall, as it is used as the police station where DI Mathias and his team are based.

Map continues on page 84

83

The view northwards before the steep descent into Borth

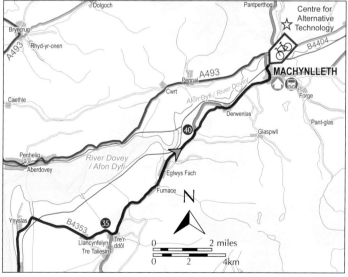

easy pedalling. Turn left in **Tre'r ddôl** (35/8 miles) and follow the A487 towards Machynlleth.

A487 SOUTH OF MACHYNLLETH

Although there is only 5 miles' of actual riding on the A487, this can be a busy road, especially at peak times, weekends and during bank holidays. Unless you are confident about taking an assertive position in the road, so traffic is forced to slow to overtake you – rather than try to squeeze by and risk forcing you into the verge – consider one of the following options:

- Take one of the frequent trains for the short journey between Borth and Machynlleth,

    or

- Ride the first 22 miles of Cross route 4 from Aberystwyth to just after Cwmystwyth. Follow NCN 818/NCN 81 to Llanidloes and then ride the final section of Cross route 3 from Llanidloes to Machynlleth; this is a journey of 54 miles, 32 miles more than the original route.

Ride through **Furnace** (37/6 miles), Eglwys Fach (38/5 miles) and Glandyfi (39/4 miles), where there is a short stretch of shared-use path. ▶ Three-quarters of a mile further on, just after passing the county boundary sign for Powys, turn right on a bend immediately after the bridge over Afon Llyfnant and follow this gated road up through the woodland and back down to rejoin the A487 by the Black Lion Inn in **Derwenlas** (41/2 miles). Turn right and join a shared-use path that goes all the way into Machynlleth where this stage ends.

Furnace gets its name from Dyfi Furnace, a now restored mid-18th-century charcoal-fired blast furnace used for smelting iron ore.

RIDING ANTICLOCKWISE

If hostels are your preferred accommodation, you may want to stop at the one in Llanrhystud, 9 miles before the end of the stage, as there aren't any other hostels near the route until after Aberporth, 34 miles further south.

MACHYNLLETH

The Victorian clock tower in the centre of Machynlleth

Although small, Machynlleth has big ambitions. Because the Welsh prince Owain Glyndŵr held a parliament here in 1404, the town claims to be the ancient capital of Wales, but in 2000 and 2002 it unsuccessfully applied for city status. It is unlikely that many of the town's residents mind because since the 1960s Machynlleth has been a magnet for those seeking an alternative lifestyle. Just off route north of Machynlleth along NCN 8 is the Centre for Alternative Technology, which was set up in an old slate quarry in 1973 to pioneer ideas about sustainable living, which are now mainstream.

Hidden in the trees above the bridge over Afon Dyfi is Bron-Yr-Aur, a privately owned 18th-century cottage where the rock band Led Zeppelin wrote and recorded part of their third album. Not everyone who came to Machynlleth stayed. But some did, setting up a wide selection of shops, cafés and small businesses that give the town its distinctive and still slightly alternative feel.

STAGE 6
Machynlleth to Porthmadog

Start	Machynlleth Railway Station (SH 745 013)
Finish	Porthmadog Railway Station (SH 566 392)
Distance	48 miles (77km)
Ascent	1100m
Time	7–8hr
OS maps	OS Landranger 124
Refreshments	Plenty, although village pubs tend to have restricted opening times with few serving lunch during the week
Accommodation	Plenty of accommodation of all types around the coast, including hostels at Barmouth and Porthmadog

This is a varied stage that crosses the Dyfi, Mawddach and Dwyryd estuaries and passes through many of the popular seaside resorts around Cardigan Bay. There are plenty of attractions, such as Harlech Castle and Portmeirion, along the way for those enjoying a more leisurely schedule.

From the station, turn right away from the town and join a shared-use path that leads to Afon Dyfi. Turn left on to the A493 after crossing Pont ar Ddyfi, following NCN 82. Turn left after 1½ miles and enjoy a short detour around a quiet lane and then rejoin the A493 and cycle through **Pennal** (3/45 miles). ▶ Turn right on the outskirts of Cwrt

While in the village in 1406 the Welsh prince Owain Glyndŵr sent the famous Pennal Letter to Charles VI of France, setting out his plans for an independent Wales.

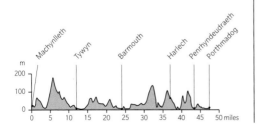

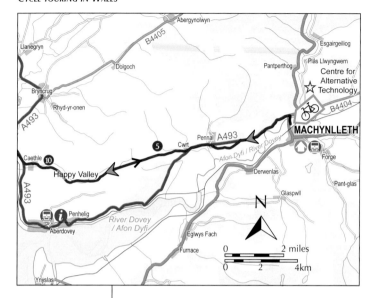

Map continues
on page 90

(4/44 miles), following signs for NCN 82 and **Happy Valley**. This is a lovely road that climbs gently up through the woods to cross a low col, where you get to feel the fresh sea air for the first time. The long descent through Cwm Maethlon is equally enjoyable, requiring limited pedalling to maintain a steady speed.

The valley is bounded by hills to the north and to the south, so you only get views out to sea on the final descent to rejoin the main road. Turn right and ride into **Tywyn** (12/36 miles) using the shared-use path that crosses over to the opposite carriageway as you approach the town. Follow marker signs for NCN 82 along Bryn Hyfryd Road and Station Road, then turn left into a minor road just before the pedestrian crossing on the High Street.

This road is a dead end for vehicles but not pedestrians or cyclists. Ride past the houses and bear right alongside the railway. After 2 miles cross the new bridge over Afon Dysynni, which connects the Broad Water tidal lagoon with the sea, and continue past Tonfanau Station

TYWYN

The construction of better roads in the early 19th century and the arrival of the railway in 1863 turned Tywyn – which in Welsh means beach or seashore – into the busy tourist destination it is today. John Corbett (1817–1901), a Midlands industrialist who made his fortune extracting and transporting salt, was responsible for much of what you see today, constructing boarding houses, a grand esplanade and the local water and sewerage systems, as well as giving land and money to build the market hall, school and assembly room. However, he never fully realized his ambition to create a grand watering-place to rival Torquay.

Slate quarrying in the hills around Abergynolwyn led to the construction of the narrow-gauge Talyllyn Railway, which opened in 1865 to carry slate down to Tywyn Wharf. Soon after commercial slate extraction ceased in 1950, a preservation society took over the line and its rolling stock, turning it into a successful and popular tourist attraction.

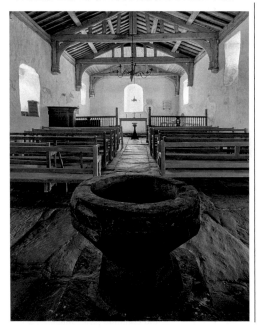

The simple interior of the ancient church at Llangelynnin

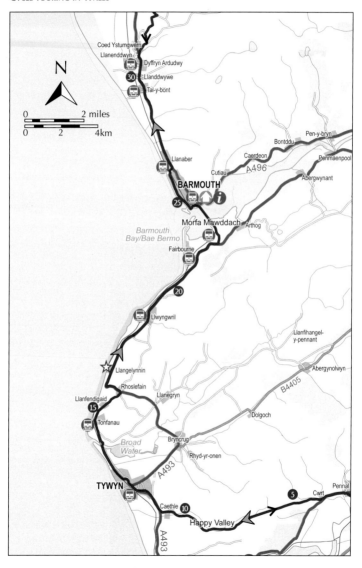

to **Rhoslefain** (16/32 miles). Look right to see Bird Rock, the distinctive, domed outcrop low on the right-hand side of the narrow Dysynni Valley. It was once a sea cliff, and despite being located 2 miles inland now, it is still used as a nesting site by seabirds, such as cormorants and chough.

Map continues on page 93

Turn left along the A493 towards Dolgellau (as it says on the sign) and continue along the coast, enjoying extensive views out across Barmouth Bay all the way around to the Llyn Peninsula. Look out for the ancient church tucked in below the road at **Llangelynnin** (17/31 miles), which retains much of its medieval character, including a wall painting.

Continue through **Llwyngwril** (19/29 miles), and then a mile after Friog (22/26 miles) turn left to join NCN 8, which stretches all the way to the Menai Bridge on Stage 7. Ride past Morfa Mawddach Station and across Barmouth Viaduct. This largely wooden viaduct, which was opened in 1867, carries the Cambrian Coast Railway across the estuary. It is a remarkable structure, but after half a mile of riding across uneven timbers you will look

Looking south from Barmouth along the viaduct across the Mawddach estuary

forward to getting off it just as much as you did to getting on it.

At its end, go through a gap in the wall, turn left and ride down Porkington Terrace into **Barmouth** (25/23 miles). Turn left on to The Quay and ride under the railway and around to The Promenade. You can enjoy traffic-free cycling on the shared-use path right along the seafront. At its end, take another shared-use path across the railway and up to join the A496. Turn left and follow this road for 4 miles, enjoying views of the Llyn Peninsula across Cardigan Bay.

Turn right in Dyffryn Ardudwy (30/18 miles) towards Cwm Nantcol and climb Ffordd-y-Briws for half a mile. Turn left following a route marker at the corner of a stone wall. Follow this narrow lane for 1 mile until you come to a junction, then turn left at the marker sign and follow

BARMOUTH

In the 16th century Barmouth was a small port used by coastal vessels trading grain, timber, wool and locally caught herring. Trade increased during the following centuries, particularly the shipping of timber used for the manufacture of pit props, and to support it Barmouth became an important centre for shipbuilding. During the 18th century local merchants built elegant Georgian homes, some of which can be seen on the town's Heritage Trail.

The town was already attracting well-to-do travellers with a fascination for picturesque landscapes, including the poet William Wordsworth (1770–1850), who after a visit in 1824, wrote, 'With a fine sea view in front, the mountains behind, the glorious estuary running eight miles inland, and Cadair Idris within compass of a day's walk, Barmouth can always hold its own against any rival.' No one could possibly disagree with him, including the holidaymakers from the industrial towns of the Midlands and North-West, who started to visit once the railway arrived in 1867. In the 20th century the traditional factory summer holiday closures brought a dramatic increase in the number of tourists, with special trains bringing thousands of factory workers and their families to the coast. Although the train still brings tourists to Barmouth today, the majority come by road, the fast A roads from the Midlands and the North West making the resort easily accessible for day-trippers.

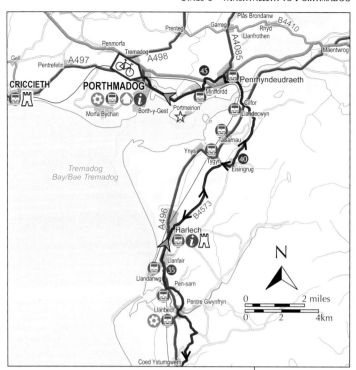

NCN 8 left and down to **Llanbedr** (33/15 miles), which is a pleasant village with both a coffee shop and a bike shop. Turn right along the A496, shortly afterwards crossing Afon Artro, and then turn right towards Cwm Bychan. Turn left by the war memorial and cycle up through the trees to meet another quiet lane that drops to rejoin the A496. Turn right on to the shared-use path and follow it into **Llanfair** (36/12 miles). From Llanfair follow Ffordd Uchaf for 1 mile, then turn right along Stryd Fawr into the centre of **Harlech** (37/11 miles), enjoying the panoramic views down across the bay.

A number of possible routes of NCN 8 criss-cross the steep hillside above Harlech, but the easiest option is to

HARLECH CASTLE

When Edward I started building Harlech Castle in 1283 during his invasion of Wales, the castle was situated on the coast, but centuries of silt deposits have left it stranded inland on a rock outcrop that was once a sea cliff. Over the centuries the castle has had many occupants. Owain Glyndŵr (1359–c.1415), the last unofficial king of Wales, captured the castle in 1404 and held it until 1409 when it was retaken by English forces. Lancastrian forces held the castle for seven years during the Wars of the Roses (1455–1487), until Yorkist troops forced them to surrender in 1468 during what is thought to have been the longest siege in the history of the British

Parked up below Harlech Castle

Isles, famously commemorated centuries later in the song 'Men of Harlech'. Forces loyal to Charles I held the castle from the outbreak of the English Civil War in 1642 until 1647, when it became the last fortification to surrender to the parliamentary armies, who subsequently destroyed the gatehouse staircases to make the castle unusable.

Since then the castle has been a picturesque ruin attracting visits from prominent landscape artists, including JMW Turner. The United Nations Educational, Scientific and Cultural Organization (UNESCO) granted the castle World Heritage status in 1986, declaring it one of 'the finest examples of late 13th-century and early 14th-century military architecture in Europe'.

From 1872 until 1997 explosives and munitions were manufactured in Penrhyndeudraeth; the site of the factory is now a nature reserve notable for nightjars in summer.

follow the B4573 northwards for 3 miles before turning right on a bend immediately after crossing Afon Y Glyn. Climb up the hillside for one-third of a mile, then turn in the tiny hamlet of Eisingrug to rejoin NCN 8. Cross the A496 at **Cilfor** and ride along the shared-use path over the River Dwyryd to **Penrhyndeudraeth**, (44/4 miles). ◀

Turn right opposite the railway station, cross the A487 at the designated crossing in the village centre and ride along Stryd Fawr for 150 metres before turning left into Pensarn opposite the village's car park. Turn left at the end of Pensarn, and then after 300 metres turn right and follow this narrow lane under the railway and the bypass and then back over the railway.

Detour to Portmeirion

If you want to visit Portmeirion, which is a round trip of 2½ miles off route, turn left at a post box, which shares an island with a fingerpost for NCN 8, by the cottages, 250 metres after passing over the railway. Cross the A487 to reach the entrance of the village.

> **Portmeirion** was built between 1925 and 1975 by local architect Clough Williams-Ellis (1883–1978). Inspired by Italian fishing villages, he also incorporated a collection of architectural relics in his design to create a picturesque village in direct contrast with the utilitarian architecture of the time. Portmeirion rocketed to fame in the late 1960s when it featured as 'The Village' in the spy drama

Portmeirion from across the Dwyryd estuary

The Prisoner. It was only then that Williams-Ellis introduced an entrance fee to prevent the village from becoming spoilt by overcrowding. He died in 1978 and in accordance with his wishes, his ashes were scattered over the estuary by a marine rocket. Today, a charitable trust runs Portmeirion, which includes a hotel, self-catering cottages, shops, a café, tea room and restaurant.

Turn right at its end and follow the shared-use path across **Britannia Terrace**, past the terminus of the Ffestiniog and Welsh Highland Railways and into Porthmadog. If you are not stopping here, turn right into Madoc Street once you pass the harbour and then immediately right along **Lynn Bach** past the town's main car park, rejoining Madoc Street once past the one-way

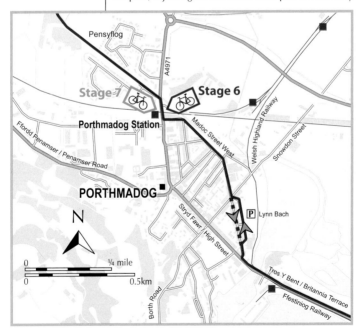

system. At the end of this road, which becomes Cambrian Terrace, turn right into High Street, and then turn left into **Pensyflog** immediately after the level crossing.

PORTHMADOG

William Madocks (1773–1828), a wealthy lawyer, acquired the Tan-yr-Allt estate on the western side of the Glaslyn estuary in 1798 and immediately commissioned a 2-mile-long embankment across the upper estuary to create productive farmland. Fuelled by his success, Madocks set about building a second, 1600-yd-long stone embankment called 'the Cob' across the lower estuary. Soon after completion in 1812, the embankment was breached in a storm and subsequent repairs left Madocks with considerable debts. Undaunted, he developed plans for a harbour at Porthmadog and a railway to Blaenau Ffestiniog, both of which came to fruition after his death when the abolition of duties on slate revitalized the industry. Today, the town that Madocks created relies on tourism for its living. The wharves survive, but the slate warehouses have been replaced by holiday apartments and the harbour is used by leisure yachts. Meanwhile, the town still celebrates William Madocks, and both of his embankments remain in use, the first carrying the Welsh Highland Railway across the estuary and the Cob carrying the A487, the Ffestiniog Railway and more recently Lôn Las Cymru.

If you want a break, bicycles can be carried on the Welsh Highland Railway, which is the UK's longest heritage railway, running for 25 miles from Porthmadog through the stunning Aberglaslyn Pass and the picture postcard village of Beddgelert and past the foot of Snowdon to Caernarfon. However, space is limited so always make a reservation before travelling, tel 01766 516024.

RIDING ANTICLOCKWISE

You can easily visit Harlech with little exertion and avoid the stretch along the B4573 by continuing south on NCN 8 until you reach the crossroads at Rhiw Goch and then descending straight down to the town. However, take care down Pen Dref, the steep hill that leads directly to the castle, as it is twisty, has gradients that at times are 20% or more and ends at a busy junction.

STAGE 7
Porthmadog to Conwy

Start	Porthmadog Railway Station (SH 566 392)
Finish	Conwy Railway Station (SH 781 775)
Distance	57 miles (91km)
Ascent	900m
Time	7–8hr
OS maps	OS Landranger 123 and 115
Refreshments	There are plenty of places for food stops, except for the 10-mile stretch between Llanystumdwy and Penygroes
Accommodation	Plenty of accommodation of all types around the coast, including hostels at Garndolbenmaen, Caernarfon and Conwy

You can easily make up lost time on this fairly flat stage, which incorporates 12 miles of traffic-free cycling along Lôn Eifion, especially if you take the waymarked shortcut through Garndolbenmaen that saves the average cyclist about 1 hour.

In the woodlands half a mile north of Golan is the Gothic 6-story Brynkir Tower built by local landowner Sir Joseph Huddart to impress the future George IV, who as Prince of Wales visited the area in 1821.

Immediately after the railway station, turn left into Pensyflog alongside a ditch that drains land reclaimed from the estuary before passing through the tunnel under the A487. At the end of this now shared-use path, turn left along Dublin Street, then quickly right into a narrow road that also quickly turns into a shared-use path and follow it past the hospital and along the hillside to **Penmorfa**. Turn right along Hen Ffordd and climb steadily uphill with views out over Cardigan Bay to your left. Turn right at the end of Hen Ffordd and continue climbing, looking back to see Moel Y Gest (863ft/263m), which despite its modest height is an impressive hill. The climbing ends near the cemetery and then the route heads briefly downhill past the woollen mill and through **Golan** (4/53), before forking left to meet the A487. ◄

Shortcut via Garndolbenmaen

If you are staying in Garndolbenmaen or need to recover lost time, there is a waymarked shortcut from just north of Porthmadog to the start of Lôn Eifion that avoids Criccieth, saving 8 miles. Turn right towards Garndolbenmaen at a fingerpost, 275 metres after passing Brynkir Woollen Mills. After three-quarters of a mile, turn left by a white cottage immediately after crossing Afon Dwyfor and follow the road past the parish church in **Dolbenmaen**. Join a shared-use path on the right just before the junction with the A487 and follow it for just less than 150 metres alongside the main road and around into the minor road that leads to **Garndolbenmaen**. Ride into Garndolbenmaen and turn right on the bend by Capel Horeb. After 1½ miles, turn right by a farm and ride for 1½ miles gently uphill along the south-western slopes of Mynydd Craig Goch (610m/2000ft). ▶ Turn left after passing the white cottage at Cwmbran and cycle downhill to meet the A487. Use the cycle path to cross the main road and then ride for half a mile across the cattle grid and towards the quarry to rejoin Lôn Las Cymru near the start of Lôn Eifion, the shared-use path that leads all the way to Caernarfon.

After assessment in 2008, this became the most westerly 2000-ft peak in Wales by a mere 5½ inches.

Map continues on page 103

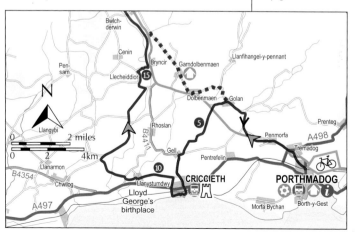

Fork left from Golan to meet the A487. Cross the junction and then after two miles turn left to join the **B4411** by a caravan park and enjoy a long descent into **Criccieth** (8/49 miles). Cross the busy A497 and then the railway line and follow the road through the village before turning

CRICCIETH CASTLE

Criccieth Castle was one of the castles built by Edward I to protect his newly won Welsh territory

It is thought that the first castle at Criccieth was built by Llywelyn the Great (Llywelyn ap Iorwerth) (c.1172–1240), who ruled most of Wales for 45 years. Much of the current structure, however, was built by Edward I at the end of the 13th century as part of a ring of castles surrounding his newly conquered Welsh lands. The rebel Owain Glyndŵr (c.1359–c.1415) briefly controlled the castle in the early years of the 15th century, but once it fell in 1404, part of the walls were torn down and both the castle and the town were burnt.

The castle was never to be reoccupied, so the town lost its importance until the arrival of the railway in 1867 gave it a new future as a resort. Notable holidaymakers included the Bird family, famous for their custard, who owned a villa opposite the lifeboat station called 'Foinavon', which the current owner has fittingly painted yellow.

right along Castle Street. After a short climb up past the castle, the road swoops downhill past the Victorian villas along Marine Crescent before turning back inland to cross the railway and the A497 at a staggered junction.

Ride up the lane, turn left at the top and ride down into **Llanystumdwy** (10/47 miles), passing the riverside grave of David Lloyd George (1863–1945).

> **Lloyd George**, the British Prime Minister from 1916 to 1922, spent much of his boyhood in the village and started his career articled to a firm of solicitors in nearby Porthmadog. You can visit the Lloyd George Museum in the centre of Llanystumdwy between April and October.

Adding a loop around the Llyn Peninsula

While the Llyn Peninsula has wonderful scenery, it also has some punishing hills and, as yet, there is no continuous, waymarked cycle route around them. But if you feel your circumnavigation is incomplete without this section, turn left just outside Llanystumdwy and follow Regional Route 40 to Chwilog (2 miles). Cross the B4354 and then 4 miles later cross the A499 at Yr Efailnewydd (8 miles). Turn left 1½ miles further on and follow Regional Route 41 to its junction with Regional Route 42 near Rhydyclafdy (10 miles). Turn left and follow Regional Route 42 through the busy resort of Abersoch to its junction with Regional Route 43, just south of Sarn Meyllteryn. Turn left and follow Regional Route 43 through Aberdaron and around the southern end of this pretty peninsula to its junction with Regional Route 42 near Porth Ychain (39 miles). Turn left

and follow Regional Route 42 through Tudweiliog (41 miles) to its junction with Regional Route 41. Turn left and follow Regional Route 41 to Nefyn (48 miles). Then follow the B4177 towards Caernarfon to Llanaelhaearn (54 miles). Turn left towards Caernarfon and follow the shared-use path northwards for 7 miles to Pontllyfni (61 miles). A mile later, turn right towards Penygroes to rejoin the route.

Incorporating the loop adds 53 miles and 1200m of ascent into the circumnavigation.

Main route continues
Turn right and cross Afon Dwyfor and then after 400 metres turn right towards Plas Talhenbont Hall, starting a gentle climb across the Llyn Peninsula. Turn left towards Llangybi a hundred metres later at an elegant lodge to the now ruined Plas Gwynfryn, a flamboyant mansion built by local landowner and MP Sir Hugh John Ellis-Nanney (1845–1920), who was defeated in the parliamentary by-election of 1890 by the young Lloyd George.

Half a mile later cross the bridge over Afon Dwyfach and follow the road past the gatehouse of the 17th-century Plas Talhenbont Hall, which is now an exclusive wedding venue. Turn right at the next junction, joining a regional cycle route and follow this winding road for 3 miles to its end. Look out for some substantial gateposts that were probably standing stones before being repurposed in the days before heritage conservation.

Turn left and follow this road for 1 mile, past a seemingly deserted farmyard at **Llecheiddior**. Turn right, ride through the evidently busy farmyard at Llecheiddior Uchaf and down the twisting concrete drive to the livestock market and industrial units on the site of the old station at **Bryncir** (16/41 miles).

From here, for 12 miles, to the end of the stage in Caernarfon, the route follows Lôn Eifion along sections of track bed of the former Caernarfonshire Railway that were not incorporated into the A487, which runs parallel. Unless there is a headwind, progress is rapid, especially if you are in a group and get into a rhythm negotiating the numerous gates. For the most part, you will be oblivious of the villages served by the line – Pant Glâs, Penygroes, Groeslon, Llanwnda, Dinas and Bontnewydd – that are just to the east. A sign on the route just after **Penygroes** (22/35 miles) directs you to the Inigo Jones Slate Works and café, which is adjacent to the route. ▶

Use the designated crossings to negotiate the busy roundabout just south of **Llanwnda** (26/31 miles). Otherwise just enjoy the views of Snowdon at the end of the Nantlle Valley to the east and the remaining few miles of traffic-free cycling into **Caernarfon** (28/29 miles).

The historic Grade I listed gardens of Glynllifon Park are 2 miles off route to the west of Groeslon.

Map continues on page 107

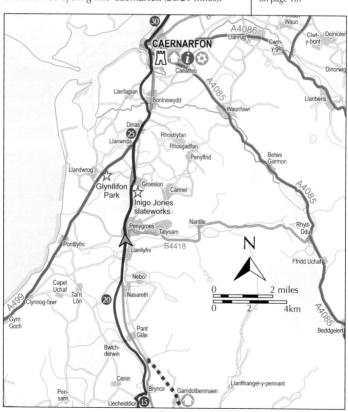

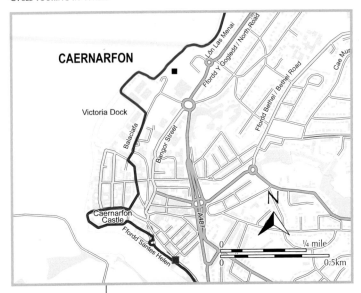

The outwardly impressive Caernarfon Castle, which dominates the town

The building of **Caernarfon Castle** was begun in 1283 during the reign of Edward I and completed in 1330 during the reign of his grandson Edward III. Although Caernarfon appears to be a well-preserved castle, none of its interior buildings has survived, and many planned buildings were never finished. When Henry VII (1457–1509) seized the English crown after the Battle of Bosworth in 1485, his Welsh ancestry help legitimize the Tudor's rule over Wales, tensions diminished and the castle fell into disrepair. Despite its dilapidated condition, it was occupied by the Royalists during the English Civil War (1642–1651) and was besieged three times before the garrison finally surrendered to the Parliamentarian forces in 1646. It was the last time Caernarfon Castle saw conflict.

The government started to fund repairs to Caernarfon Castle in the late Victorian era, since when it has become the recognized location for the investiture of the title of Prince of Wales on the British monarch's heir.

Cycle around the castle, through the archway and up Castle Ditch. As you approach Castle Square, turn left down Greengate Street alongside the town walls, underneath the Eastgate archway and down Bank Quay. Turn right into Glan Mor opposite North Gate and ride along **Balaclafa Road**, joining a shared-use path that leads around the perimeter of Victoria Dock car park and northwards along the coast. The route then joins **Lôn Las Menai**, a 4-mile section of dismantled railway that linked Caernarfon with the old slate harbour of Y Felinheli (Port Dinorwic). It is pleasant cycling through broadleaf woodlands, briefly emerging to follow a shared-use path alongside and then parallel to the old Caernarfon Road before emerging on Beach Road in **Y Felinheli** (33/24 miles).

Turn left and ride down through the industrial units to the little seafront. Turn left at the corner by the Garddfon Inn and follow the route through the houses, along Hen Gei Llechi and past the old port, which is now a busy marina. Turn left on to the cycle path just before the T-junction with the main Bangor road, then cross the main road, again following the course of the old railway.

Within a mile the route rejoins the road. Turn left at the T-junction with the **B4547**, take the shared-use path on the opposite carriageway and keep right at the next junction, following signs towards Bangor. Soon you have to cross to a shared-use path that runs along the opposite carriageway adjacent to the walls of Vaynol Hall.

> Owner of the **Vaynol Estate**, Thomas Assheton Smith (1752–1828) became fabulously wealthy from slate quarrying. Early in the 19th century he developed the Dinorwic Quarry near Llanberis, but it never flourished until he constructed a horse-drawn tramway to Port Dinorwic in 1824.
>
> Later that century, when steam trains carried the slate, Dinorwic Quarry employed more than 3000 men and was the second largest opencast slate producer in the country. Production dwindled during the 20th century and finally ceased in 1969. Likewise, the Assheton Smith family, which had amassed 36,000 acres of land by the start of the 20th century, gradually disposed of their estate and finally sold Vaynol Hall in 1984.

Cross again after the roundabout, following a path alongside the A487. At the top of the rise, turn right and ride over the A55 Expressway and into Penrhos Garnedd (35/22 miles), before turning left at a mini roundabout. Turn right on the first bend, following route markers into an unnamed lane. Then at its end, turn right towards Bangor, following a shared-use path alongside the opposite carriageway. As you descend towards the **Menai Straits**, the path narrows, so briefly join the road then rejoin the shared-use path once past the roundabout.

Adding a loop around Anglesey
If you wish to add a loop around the island of Anglesey, cross the Menai Suspension Bridge and follow NCN 8

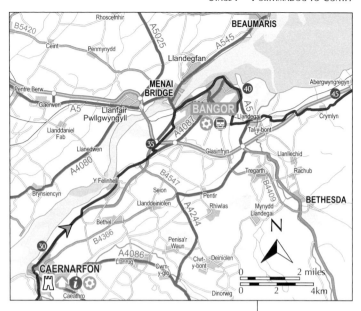

to Valley (26 miles). Then follow NCN 5 until its junction with NCN 566 near Llanddeusant (33 miles), before turning left to follow NCN 566 around the north of the island until it rejoins NCN 5 at Llanerchymedd (60 miles). Finally, follow NCN 5 through Menai Bridge Town (80 miles) and back across the Menai Suspension Bridge to rejoin the route. Although the amount of climbing is negligible, you should still add two extra days on to your schedule.

Continue into **Bangor** (38/19 miles) on the shared-use path, enjoying views of Anglesey across the Menai Straight. Keep straight ahead if you need to go into the city centre. Otherwise, bear left on a bend, leaving the A5 to follow NCN 5 down **Ffordd Siliwen**. This soon turns into a quiet lane and leads around Garth Point with fine views out to sea. ▶

Map continues on page 110

The Grade II listed Garth Pier, the second longest in Wales after nearby Llandudno, was opened in 1896 and once handled pleasure steamers cruising to and from Blackpool, Liverpool and the Isle of Man.

107

MENAI SUSPENSION BRIDGE

Thomas Telford's Menai Suspension Bridge viewed from across the Menai Strait

Before the Menai Suspension Bridge opened in 1826, the only way to and from Anglesey was by taking the ferry across the fast-flowing and dangerous waters of the Menai Strait. One of the most tragic accidents occurred in 1785, when 54 passengers drowned after a boat became stranded on a sandbar. Valuable cattle raised on Anglesey also frequently perished as drovers swam them across on their way to mainland markets.

Eventually Thomas Telford (1757–1834) was commissioned to find a solution, and he proposed a suspension bridge that would avoid having to build piers on the shifting sands of the seabed and which would be high enough to allow ships to pass beneath. The bridge has been strengthened many times to make it more stable in high winds and to cope with increased traffic. The growth in rail travel necessitated building the nearby Britannia Bridge, which was designed and built by the engineer Robert Stephenson (1803–1859) and opened in 1850. Although it now carries the majority of today's traffic, it lacks the elegance of Telford's bridge, which is a Grade I listed building and World Heritage Site. Even George Borrow, who was usually disdainful of technological advances like the railway, called it 'a most beautiful suspension bridge… the result of the mental and manual labours of the ingenious Telford'. However, he soon returned to character, writing that Stephenson's Britannia Bridge was 'a wonderful structure, but anything but graceful'.

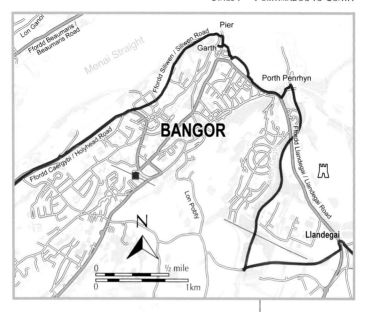

Soon after passing through Garth, turn left and follow NCN 5 waymarker signs down a narrow lane to the sea-front, along Beach Road and left towards Porth Penrhyn, following a shared-use path alongside the A5. Bear left immediately before the causeway, then turn right once across Afon Cegin. Follow the shared-use path upstream for 1¼ miles then leave the river, turn right and cross back over the path on the bridge. Follow waymarker signs for NCN 5 across the busy A5, around the village of **Llandygai** (42/15 miles) and over Afon Ogwen.

In the late 19th century **Porth Penrhyn** was the main port for the export of slate from the Penrhyn Quarry. It was then the largest slate quarry in the world, creating huge wealth for the Pennant family of nearby Penrhyn Castle, which is now in the care of the National Trust.

109

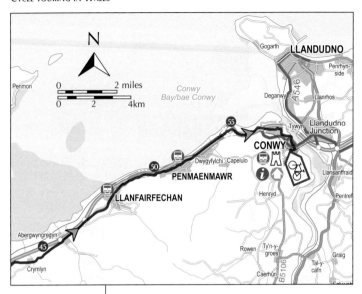

Turn left at the next junction and then right towards
Rachub immediately after crossing over the railway. A
few hundred metres later turn left by a small church and
then at its end rejoin the original road, which was once
the main turnpike between Chester and Holyhead, by
a squat tollhouse. Bear left and cross the North Wales
Expressway, then immediately left again by a well-preserved Victorian farmyard that was built by the Penrhyn
Estate in 1860 for breeding and training horses.

Follow waymarker sign through **Abergwyngregyn**
(46/11 miles) and the former seaside resorts of
Llanfairfechan (48/9 miles) and **Penmaenmawr** (51/6
miles), where NCN 5 follows a shared-use path that
snakes its way high above the A55 around Penmaen-bach
Point. Good views right around Conwy Bay take in the
north-eastern corner of Anglesey and Puffin Island, where
the eradication of predators has boosted the number of
breeding puffins and the Great Orme. As you approach
Conwy, turn right following waymarker signs towards

CONWY

Cyclists crossing the road bridge at Conwy

Edward I built Conwy Castle and the town walls between 1283 and 1289 to strengthen his control over the local population; those born inside the walls today are nicknamed Jackdaws after the birds that live on them. For centuries a ferry crossed the strongly tidal River Conwy, but it ceased to operate in 1826 with the building of Thomas Telford's suspension bridge, which has supporting towers designed to match the castle's turrets. The engineer Robert Stephenson completed the tubular railway bridge in 1849, and since 1991 the busy A55 has passed below the river through an immersed tube tunnel, relieving the town of considerable traffic. There is plenty to see in Conwy, including Plas Mawr, a fine Elizabethan house built in 1576; the smallest house in Great Britain; and The Albion, a Grade II listed art nouveau pub of 1921, which is jointly operated by four North Wales craft breweries.

Conwy Marina, cross the busy coastal expressway and then turn left along a shared-use path that runs along the estuary to Conwy where the stage ends.

RIDING ANTICLOCKWISE

If you start out early, you could easily ride well beyond Porthmadog as this stage is remarkably flat.

STAGE 8
Conwy to Wrexham

Start	Conwy Railway Station (SH 781 775)
Finish	Wrexham General Railway Station (SJ 329 508)
Distance	65 miles (104km)
Ascent	800m
Time	8–9hr
OS maps	OS Landranger 115, 116 and 117
Refreshments	Ample places to stop along the coast but much less choice inland
Accommodation	The only hostel is early in the stage at Llandudno, but there are plenty of hotels, guest houses and B&Bs along the coast and near the end of the stage in Wrexham

Other than a short climb over Halkyn Mountain, which is essential to avoid the busy coast road, this stage is remarkably flat. There are plenty of big expansive views to enjoy, first along the north coast and then down across the Wirral to Liverpool, before reaching the flatter farmland towards the end of the stage.

Follow the one-way system around the town and cross the river using the shared-use path. Swing left on the opposite bank following NCN 5 through Deganwy and along a gravelly and sometimes sandy path, where you will need to dismount, until you reach West Parade. Turn

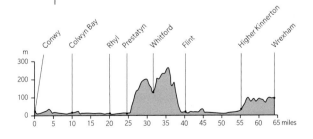

LLANDUDNO

A lone cyclist climbs the zig-zags on the way to the summit of the Great Orme

Until the arrival of the railway in 1848, many of the inhabitants of Llandudno worked in local copper mines, in fishing and in subsistence agriculture. All that changed when Owen Williams, an architect and surveyor from Liverpool, presented local landowner, Lord Mostyn, with plans to develop the marshlands behind Llandudno Bay as a holiday resort, resulting in much of what you see today.

By 1864 Llandudno was already being advertised as the 'Queen of the Welsh Resorts', and later attractions such as the town's Grade II listed pier, which was built in 1878 and extended inland in 1884 to make it the longest in Wales, cemented its popularity. The town's busy calendar of events and easy access by road mean it is always thronged with day-trippers whenever the sun comes out. But the town's mild climate and well-preserved, elegant buildings also make it a popular place to retire, helping the local economy through the quieter winter months.

The Great Orme (679ft/207m) is a haven for wildlife, including a species of wild cotoneaster that is only found there. The sheer limestone cliffs provide ideal nesting conditions for a wide variety of seabirds, including cormorants, shags, guillemots, razorbills, puffins, kittiwakes, fulmars and a number of different gulls. You can ride around the one-way loop to its summit where there is a popular café, but be prepared for a couple of steep ramps near the top.

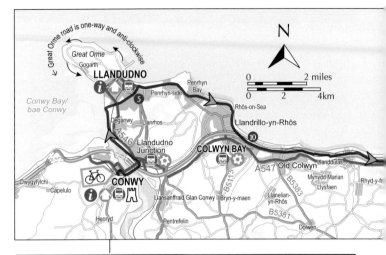

GWRYCH CASTLE

High in the woods above Abergele is Gwrych Castle, a Grade I listed 19th-century country house that has a chequered history but a happy ending. It was built between 1812 and 1822 by Lloyd Hesketh Bamford-Hesketh. His granddaughter, Winifred Bamford-Hesketh, Countess of Dundonald (1859–1924) had been unhappily married to Lt General Douglas Cochrane, and after she inherited the Gwrych Estate in 1894 she eventually banished him from the castle and immersed herself in charitable works. In her will she left the estate to King George V and the Prince of Wales, so that the Royal Family could have a permanent base in Wales. However, her request was turned down and her exiled husband bought the Castle. During World War II it was used to house refugees and subsequently had a string of different owners and many different uses, including the most recent initiative to convert the slowly deteriorating castle into a luxury hotel, which failed.

The white knight who came to its rescue was local boy Mark Baker, who as an eleven-year-old in 1996 passed the castle daily on his way to school. Appalled by the destruction, he founded the precursor of the Gwrych Castle Preservation Trust at the age of 12, pursued a career as an architectural historian and saw his dream come true when the trust he helped to establish acquired Gwrych Castle and its estate in 2018 with the help of a grant from

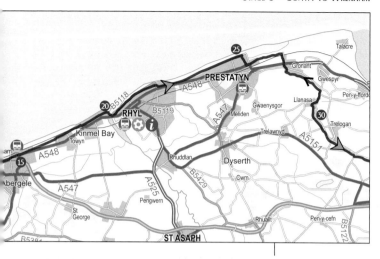

the National Heritage Memorial Fund. It is a fairy tale come true but not yet with a happy ending, as there is considerable work still to be done to renovate the castle and its 250 acres of park and woodland. Meanwhile, the castle and grounds are currently open daily to visitors, but sections of the main building remain closed due to its derelict state.

inland towards **Llandudno**, still following NCN 5, and make use of shared-use paths along Bryniau Road and Maesdu Road until you arrive on the promenade.

Other than a short climb up Penrhyn Hill behind Little Orme's Head, the next 20 miles are almost entirely flat and the miles through **Rhos-on-Sea** (9/56 miles), **Colwyn Bay** (11/54 miles), Abergele (17/48 miles), **Rhyl** (21/44 miles) and **Prestatyn** (24/41 miles) fly by quickly, a blur of sea-side resorts, caravan parks and wide open spaces. ▸

After Prestatyn, follow NCN 5 inland across the golf course before turning right alongside a popular caravan park. Cross the main A548 and then climb up through Upper Gronant (28/37 miles), **Llanasa** (30/35 miles) and past Berthengam before briefly dropping down into **Whitford** (33/32miles), from where you can see the

Map continues on page 117

Offshore is Gwynt y Môr (Sea Wind), the second largest operating offshore windfarm in the world, capable of powering a third of Welsh homes.

115

FLINT CASTLE

Flint Castle was the first of what would become known as Edward I's Iron Ring – a chain of fortresses built to control the Welsh. One of its corner towers is enlarged and isolated to form a secure keep, much like the Savoyard castles that Edward may have seen when he passed through France to join the Eighth Crusade in 1270.

It was here on 13 August 1399 that the hugely unpopular Richard II (1367–1400) surrendered to his arch-enemy Henry Bolingbroke (1367–1413), promising to abdicate if his life was spared. Henry, who subsequently became Henry IV, the first King of England from the Lancaster branch of the Plantagenets, honoured this agreement but locked Richard in the Tower of London. However, when the guilt-ridden Henry discovered a plot by Richard's supporters to rescue him and restore him to the throne, he had him removed to Pontefract Castle in Yorkshire. By 14th February 1400, less than six months after he was overthrown, Richard was either secretly murdered or, as was believed at the time, he died of starvation, either due to his own refusal to eat or to the deliberate neglect of his gaolers acting under orders from above. Mathe, Richard's once faithful greyhound, is said to have sensed his master's downfall by readily licking Henry's hand on their first meeting.

The castle was destroyed by the Parliamentarians after they captured it from the Royalists during the English Civil War in 1647. Today, it stands somewhat forlorn, trapped between the heavily silted estuary and the modern town that grew up behind it.

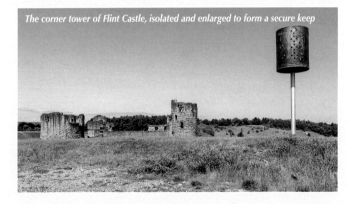

The corner tower of Flint Castle, isolated and enlarged to form a secure keep

iconic buildings of Liverpool on a clear day. ▶ Continue climbing through Pantasaph (35/30miles), across the A55 and through Calcoed and **Brynford** (37/28 miles).

Just after Brynford turn left, still following NCN 5, to drop down to the coast at Bagillt (41/24 miles). Turn left and follow NCN 5 on shared-use paths and quiet side roads through **Flint** (42/23 miles), the housing estates of Connah's Quay (47/18miles) and the industrial estate behind Shotton to the Dee Estuary.

Cross the river, turn right on the opposite bank and head south along the shared-use path towards Chester, briefly emerging on to the road to cross Station Road in **Queensferry** near the Jubilee Bridge. The route never

Although his remains have never been discovered, an engraved stone slab from the tomb of Gruffudd Fychan, (c.1330–1369), father of the Welsh rebel Owain Glyndŵr, survives in Llanasa church.

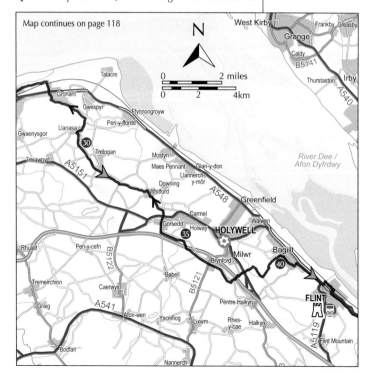

Map continues on page 118

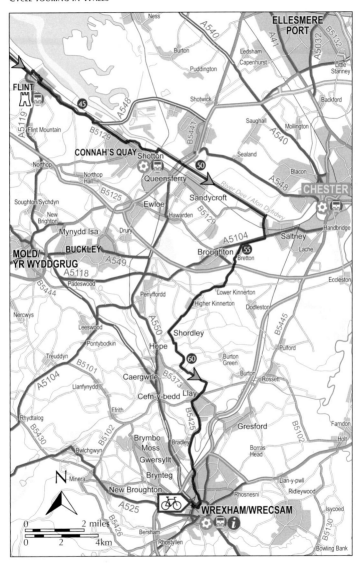

enters England as the land reclaimed in the 1730s when Dutch engineers straightened the river remains part of Wales despite being on the eastern bank of the River Dee. If you want to visit or stay in Chester, which is only 2½ miles upstream, stick on the shared-use path. Otherwise, cross the footbridge at Saltney Ferry (53/12 miles), join the B5129 on the opposite bank and cross the railway to meet the A5014. Turn right and follow the shared-use path alongside the opposite carriage, then turn left in **Bretton** (54/11 miles). Ride through the village, over the A55 and into **Lower Kinnerton**. Turn right and ride through Higher Kinnerton (57/8 miles). ▶

Turn left into Shordley Road, a mile beyond the village, go straight on at the next crossroads and ride through **Shordley**, which consists of a large farm and a few cottages. Enjoy the fine view across the Cheshire Plain towards the low hills that form the backbone of the Sandstone Trail. Turn left towards Golly at the next junction. A mile further on, where signs on the verge mark where Dark Lane becomes Higher Lane, turn right into Chapel Lane. Turn right again at the traffic lights at the end of this lane and ride into **Llay** (62/3 miles). Turn left towards Bradley at the mini roundabout by the Miners Welfare Institute, which remains the social hub of the village despite the local colliery closing in 1966. ▶ Pick up the shared-use path that runs alongside the B5425 and follow this to Rhosrobin, then join the road and ride through Rhosddu into the centre of **Wrexham**. If you are heading for the station, cross the inner ring road into Rhosddu Road, and then follow the cycle route signs right into King Street and around the one-way system to the end of this stage.

Lower Kinnerton has a number of Grade II listed farmhouses with distinctive Dutch gables built by the 1st Duke of Westminster in the 1890s.

Llay was built as a garden village to house the families of 2500 miners who worked in local collieries during the interwar years.

RIDING ANTICLOCKWISE

Cyclists can ride the one-way loop around the Great Orme for free. There is no need to battle all the way to the summit. Start behind the Grand Hotel and ride round below the cliffs and then continue along the coast to Deganwy and rejoin NCN 5 for the final 3 miles into Conwy.

WREXHAM

With the coming of the Industrial Revolution in the second half of the 18th century, local deposits of coal and ironstone meant that Wrexham was transformed from a small market town into the metropolis of North Wales. Before World War I, 10,000 people were employed in the North-East Wales coal field and thousands more in the iron and steel industry, with others employed in ancillary industries, such as brewing the town's famous lager, which was first manufactured by German immigrants in 1881.

By the end of the 1970s all of the heavy industry had closed, replaced in part by lighter manufacturing, bio-technology and distribution, concentrated on a large industrial estate to the south of the town. Wrexham lager is seeing a resurgence, and it is being brewed again at a new, hi-tech brewery that opened in 2011 after the original brewery closed in 2000.

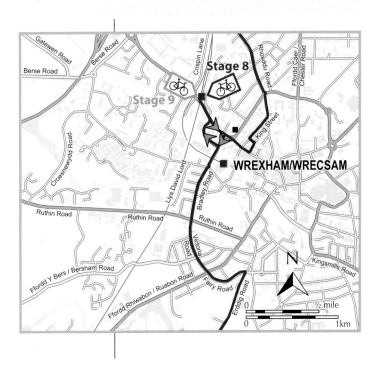

STAGE 9

Wrexham to Montgomery

Start	Wrexham General Railway Station (SJ 329 508)
Finish	Montgomery below the Castle (SO 223 970)
Distance	50 miles (80km)
Ascent	900m
Time	6–7hr
OS maps	OS Landranger 117, 126, 136 and 137
Refreshments	Plenty of places to stop in the towns, but not so many in rural areas, especially along the 21-mile stretch between Oswestry and Welshpool
Accommodation	The only hostel is off route early in the stage at Llangollen, but there is plenty of other types of accommodation, especially in the towns along the way

This stage makes use of the flat marcher country on the English side of the border before climbing Long Mountain, which provides wonderful views eastwards to the Midlands and westwards into the Cambrian Mountains. There are plenty of attractions along the way, including crossing the historic Pontcysyllte Aqueduct and visiting Powis Castle, which is just off route near Welshpool.

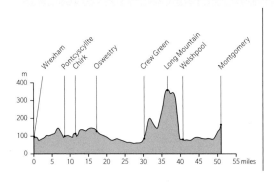

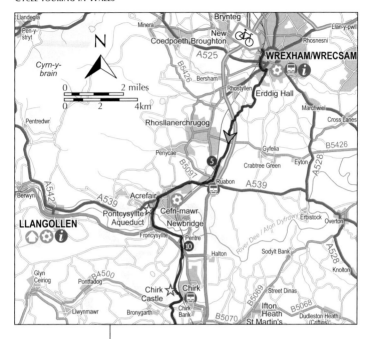

Map continues
on page 125

Head along Regents Street towards the town centre and then turn right on to the inner ring road at the traffic lights, following signs for Whitchurch. After 1 mile turn right off the tree-lined Fairy Road into Erddig Road and ride into Erddig Park. Pass **Erddig Hall** and bear right, taking the exit route to the right of the giant conifers.

> **Erddig Hall**, which was built in the 1680s, became seriously unstable when a mine shaft at a nearby colliery collapsed in the 1960s, creating 5 feet of subsidence. Philip Yorke (1905–1978), whose family had lived at Erddig since 1733, gifted the property to the National Trust for restoration on the condition that nothing was to be removed from the house. The Yorke family rarely threw anything away, so today the house has a unique collection

of both rare objects and everyday items, including many belonging to the family's much-loved staff. This eclecticism makes it one of the UK's favourite historic houses.

Turn left at the gatehouse and follow the blue cycle route marker along Hafod Road and New Hall Road to **Ruabon** (5/45 miles). ▶ Turn left along the High Street and then just after passing through the village centre, turn right into Wynnstay Gardens and follow a shared-use path alongside the railway. Turn right along the **A539**, soon picking up another shared-use path that leads across the main road and into the residential estate opposite. Ride along Hampden Way and Oak Road and then rejoin the main road.

Ride downhill through **Acrefair** (7/44 miles) and turn left down Tower Hill, following signs for canal boat trips and then turn right near its end along a track that leads to the canal. Bear left to join the towpath at the busy Trevor Basin, dismount to cross **Pontcysyllte Aqueduct** (8/42 miles) and then follow the towpath through Whitehouse Tunnel into **Chirk** (12/38 miles). ▶

The Redbrick universities founded in the early 20th century got their nickname from the terracotta bricks that were made in Ruabon for over 130 years.

Use lights through Whitehouse Tunnel, which was one of the first in the UK to have a towpath, as is dark, narrow and often busy with walkers.

Crossing the Pontcysyllte Aqueduct

Cyclists park up against the magnificent iron gates at Chirk Castle, which were made at a forge near Wrexham between 1719 and 1721

The entrance to 13th-century Chirk Castle, the only one of Edward I's fortresses still inhabited today, is just quarter of a mile from Chirk Station.

Engineers Thomas Telford and William Jessop built **Pontcysyllte Aqueduct** to carry the Llangollen Canal over the River Dee. The aqueduct, which was opened to boats in 1805, is 307m long and consists of a series of locally manufactured cast-iron troughs supported on 18 hollow masonry piers that stand 126ft (38m) above the river. Today, the structure is a Grade I listed building and a World Heritage Site.

However, it is something of an expensive folly, as finances ran out and plans to extend the canal from the basin at the northern end of the aqueduct into the industrial valleys around Wrexham and beyond to Liverpool had to be abandoned. This necessitated the construction of the narrow branch canal to Llangollen, which was only built to supply water from the River Dee.

Leave the towpath at Chirk Tunnel, cross the railway and turn immediately right into Station Road. ◄ At its end, turn right on to the B4500 towards Dolywern. After half a mile turn left at the first bridge over Afon Ceiriog.

Bear left, climb up the hillside and ride into **Weston Rhyn** (13/37 miles). Bear right at the five-way junction in the centre of the village, heading towards Selattyn. After 300 metres, turn left towards Middle Hengoed and follow this lane across the next few crossroads. A further 500 metres after crossing the road between **Gobowen** and Selattyn, turn right at a three-way junction around a triangular patch of grass and ride past the impressive grassy ramparts of the Iron Age hill fort to **Oswestry** (17/33 miles). ▶

Turn left in Wat's Drive at the mini roundabout and follow the road round into Coppice Drive. At its end, cross into Whittington Road, passing under the railway and then turn immediately right into Unicorn Road. Cross the staggered junction by the convenience store into College Road and then turn left along Shrewsbury Road, following a shared-use path alongside the opposite carriageway. Turn right after one-third of a mile, ride through the industrial

Old Oswestry, as the fort is known, was occupied from 800BC until sometime in the 1st century AD and remains one of the best preserved examples in the UK.

Map continues on page 126

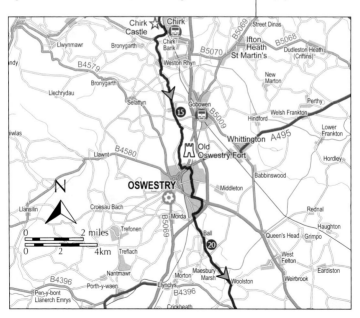

Map continues
on page 129

The Grade I listed
black and white,
timber-framed
church in Melverley
was built in 1406
to replace one the
rebellious Welsh
prince Owain
Glyndŵr burnt
down in 1401.

estate and then turn left and cross the A483 using a short
stretch of cycle path, following signs for Maesbury.

Ride through Maesbury (21/29 miles), **Maesbury
Marsh** and Woolston and then turn left into Knockin
(24/26 miles). In the centre of the village turn right towards
Kinnerley and then turn right in **Kinnerley** (25/25 miles)
towards Edgerley. After 2¼ miles, turn right towards
Melverley, joining NCN 81, which the stage follows for
the next 22 miles. Turn left, ride through Melverley
(29/21 miles), cross the River Severn and then turn right along the
B4393 towards **Crew Green**. ◄ Since leaving Chirk, the
route has kept to the flatter ground on the English side of
the border, but now back in Wales, things get a bit lumpier.

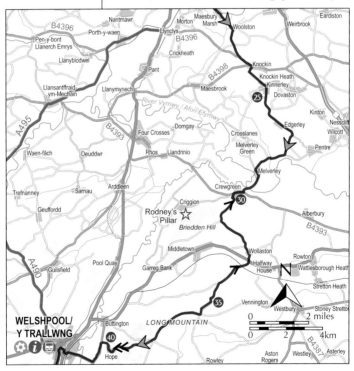

Turn left in Crew Green (30/20 miles), following NCN 81 waymarkers, and climb through the low hills before descending to **Wollaston** (33/17 miles), looking back northwards to see the flat country you have now left behind. The monument on nearby Breidden Hill was erected to commemorate the victories of Admiral George Rodney (1718–1792), whose fleet was built of local oak shipped down the River Severn to naval dockyards at Bristol. Cross the A483 and the railway, then just over a mile later turn left towards Rowley. The next mile is the steepest part of the long ascent of **Long Mountain**, with gradients touching double figures. At the top, turn right along the broad ridge and enjoy the well-earned views. If you want a shortcut that saves 5 miles by missing out Welshpool, follow signs for Forden and from there signs for Montgomery.

Rodney's Pillar on Breidden Hill was erected to commemorate the victories of Admiral George Rodney (1718–1792), whose fleet was built of local oak

Otherwise, follow NCN 81 waymarkers right at the next junction for an exhilarating descent through Hope (38/12 miles). Turn left along the B4388 and then right into **Welshpool** (42/8 miles), first crossing the River Severn and then passing the town's station. Follow road signs for the town centre and then half way along Seven Street, drop down to the Montgomery Canal just before the bridge by the Powysland Museum.

WELSHPOOL

The Welsh name for Welshpool is Y Trallwng, which means 'the marshy or sinking land', reflecting its position on a rise above the broad valley of the River Severn. Agriculture has always been important to Welshpool, and the town's livestock auction holds the largest one-day sheep sale in Europe. One of the town's most interesting buildings also has an agricultural connection; the octagonal Old Cockpit, which is set back behind the car park on New Street, is unique in Wales as the only surviving cockpit still on its original site. It is thought to have been built in the middle of the 18th century, and it remained in use until cock-fighting was made illegal in 1849.

Powis Castle, which can be seen from the B4388 on the wooded hillside to the south of the town, is a more attractive building. Built by a Welsh prince in the 13th century, the castle passed through a succession of owners until it was inherited by the Herbert family during the reign of George II. In 1784 Lady Henrietta Herbert married Edward Clive (1754–1839), the eldest son of Clive of India (1725–1774). Like his father, Edward had worked in the East India Company and had a substantial fortune that enabled the castle and its famous terraced gardens to be substantially improved. In accordance with an earlier will under which the Herbert family had inherited the castle, Edward's son changed his name to Herbert, maintaining the name of the family that still owns the castle today. To visit the castle, which is half a mile off the route, leave the canal at bridge number 120.

Follow the towpath for 6 miles until you reach The Nags Head at **Garthmyl** (47/3 miles). The Montgomery Canal was built between 1790 and 1819 and carried locally quarried limestone and coal from the North Shropshire coalfield to canal-side kilns that produced quicklime, which was used as fertiliser.

Leave the towpath at bridge 131, where the canal disappears underground in a culvert, turn right along the A483 towards Newtown and then left on the B4385 towards Montgomery. Cross the River Severn, then the railway, enjoying the views of Shropshire Hills to the east, and then climb the short hill up into **Montgomery** where this stage ends.

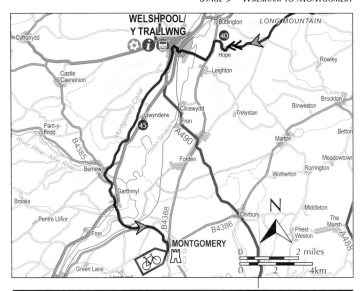

MONTGOMERY

The Norman Roger de Montgomery (1005–1094) built the first motte and bailey castle at Montgomery to control an important ford across the River Severn. It was rebuilt in stone a mile to the south-east of the original site during the 13th century. The Welsh Prince Owain Glyndŵr sacked the town at the beginning of the 15th century, but the garrison withstood his attack and the castle survived. Like many castles, it was demolished during the English Civil War after its then owner, the Royalist Edward Herbert, surrendered to Parliamentarian troops.

For the next two centuries Montgomery prospered as an important commercial centre and the county town of Montgomeryshire. But once the railway arrived at nearby Newtown and Welshpool in the middle of the 19th century, Montgomery lost much of its commercial importance. When Montgomeryshire was absorbed into Powys during the local authority reorganization in 1974, the town lost its role as an administrative centre. Many would say it was all to the good, as Montgomery has retained an unspoilt feel and has some fine examples of Georgian and early Victorian architecture, which are detailed on discrete information panels attached to each building.

This thriving general store in Montgomery stocks inner tubes and other essentials for cyclists

RIDING ANTICLOCKWISE

The climb from the B4388 to the top of Long Mountain stretches for 2 miles at an average gradient of 8%. Although the views from the summit out across the Shropshire plain are stunning, you can avoid the climb by continuing northwards along the B4388 to Buttington, turning right along the A458 towards Shrewsbury and then right again into Heldre Lane a mile further on. Follow this lane along the foot of Long Mountain for 3½ miles to rejoin NCN 81.

STAGE 10
Montgomery to Hay-on-Wye

Start	Montgomery, below the Castle (SO 223 970)
Finish	Hay-on-Wye, below the Castle (SO 231 423)
Distance	48 miles (77km)
Ascent	1300m
Time	8–9hr
OS maps	OS Landranger 137,136 and 148
Refreshments	Unless you make a detour into Sarn, which is just half a mile off route, there is nothing for the first 14 miles until Beguildy, after which there are plenty of choices in the main towns but nothing in between
Accommodation	There are hostels at Kington, near the end of the stage, and at Glasbury, which is 4 miles off route at the end of the stage. There are plenty of other choices in the major centres

This stage straddles the border, passing through glorious countryside between the historic market towns of Knighton, Presteigne and Kington. After Beguildy there are plenty of places to top up the energy levels for a couple of steady climbs that give superb views over and across the countryside below, making for a memorable day.

Leave the town, heading south on the **B4385** towards Bishop's Castle and then turn right into Back Lane alongside the Crown Inn. Turn left at its end and then left again into Kerry Road, which runs along the hills giving excellent views across to the Long Mynd and neighbouring hills across the border in Shropshire.

After 1 mile turn right towards Cefn-Y-Coed and then left at the next junction towards Sarn. After 500 metres turn left at a crossroads opposite the driveway to Gate Farm and follow this narrow lane for 1 mile. Immediately after passing a large farm, turn right by a

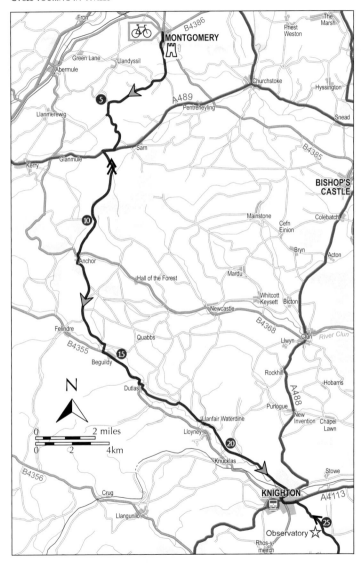

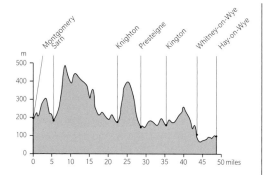

white cottage and then quickly left to meet the **A489** (6/42 miles).

Turn right, and then quickly left, climb up Kerry Hill and ride through Ceri Forest where foragers will find a feast of wild bilberries alongside the road in summer. Cross the B4368 and ride past the remote Anchor Inn (10/38 miles), an old drovers' pub that regretfully only opens in the evenings, then turn right and descend the slopes of Black Mountain to meet the B4355. Turn left towards Knighton and ride through **Beguildy** (15/33 miles). ▸ Turn left immediately before **Dutlas** (16/32 miles), cross the River Teme and follow the quieter road along the opposite bank through **Llanfair Waterdine** (18/30 miles) to meet NCN 825 for the final few miles into **Knighton** (22/26 miles).

Knighton (the knight's town) grew to become an important centre for the wool trade during the 15th century and later became an important stopping place on drovers' routes. Today, the town is a commercial centre for a large rural hinterland and for seasonal visitors, including many who come to walk Glyndŵr's Way or Offa's Dyke Path, which both pass through the town. The Spaceguard Centre, next to the route to the south of Knighton, is a working observatory that tracks near-Earth objects, such as asteroids and comets that come

The Shropshire author Mary Webb (1881–1927), who is often compared with Dorset's Thomas Hardy, used Beguildy, Sarn and other local place names for characters in her novels, which were hugely popular during her lifetime.

Map continues on page 135

close to, and sometimes collide with, the Earth. It is open from Wednesday to Sunday but has no catering facility.

Follow NCN 825 waymarkers through the town and out along the A 4113, then turn right in Llanshay Lane, following a brown sign for The Spaceguard Centre. Climb gently up Reeves Hill, turn right near the top, still following signs for NCN 825, and enjoy the descent, taking care on sections where gravel sometimes predominates over solid tarmac. At the bottom turn left towards Presteigne and then right half a mile later. Cross the bridge over the River Lugg and ride into **Presteigne** (29/19 miles).

The Radnor Building, notable for its Arts-and-Crafts-style timber facade and colourful plasterwork, is one of many interesting buildings in Presteigne

Presteigne (the priests' town) was the county town and administrative centre of Radnorshire until these roles switched to neighbouring Llandrindod Wells at the end of the 19th century. However, its heritage and the beautiful, unspoilt countryside that surround the town have enabled it to become a

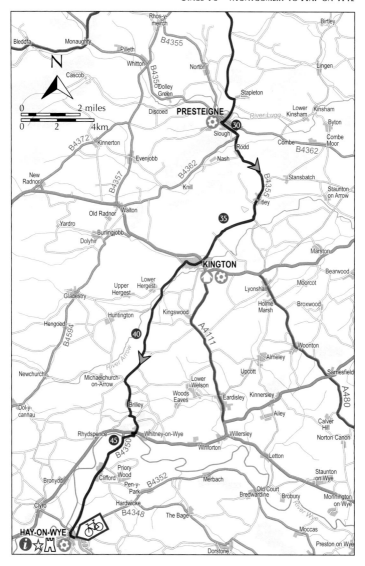

thriving tourist destination, attracting visitors with a busy calendar of events, including an annual, week-long music and arts festival at the end of August.

Keep following NCN 825 waymarkers out of the town along the B4355 and ride through Titley (33/15 miles) to **Kington** (36/12 miles).

Despite being to the west of Offa's Dyke, which until the 8th century was the border between Wales and England, **Kington** (king's town) today is in Herefordshire. Much like Knighton, it too grew up on wool-trading and droving, which is why so many long-distance trails pass through Kington today. The town still has a regular livestock market, a weekly country produce market and a monthly arts and crafts market, as well as seasonal food fares.

Ride out of the town along Church Road and then at the top of the hill turn left into Hergest Road towards Brilley. The wooded whale-back of Hergest Ridge, which forms the border between England and Wales, is above you to the west. Just after passing Hergest Court, a magnificent manor house that was once surrounded by a moat, NCN 825 turns right, but our route continues along this pleasantly rolling road to **Brilley** (42/6 miles).

Turn sharply left after descending through the woodland on the edge of the village and then right at the next junction. Follow this narrow lane past Whitney Court and down to meet the A438 at **Whitney-on-Wye** (43/5 miles). Turn right along the main road and then after 600 metres turn left towards Hay. Cross the toll bridge over the River Wye, which, like the neighbouring toll house, is a Grade II listed building. Follow this pleasantly rolling road through Clifford (46/2 miles) to **Hay-on-Wye**.

Hay-on-Wye (Y Gelli Gandryll) owes its popularity to bookseller and self-proclaimed 'King of Hay', Richard Booth, who in the 1970s pioneered

the selling of second-hand and specialist books as a way of boosting the town's economy. It was an inspired move and today the town has numerous bookshops, specialist retailers and eateries, and its annual literary festival is internationally renowned.

The bookshop of Richard Booth MBE, the self-proclaimed 'King of Hay', who did much to establish Hay-on-Wye as a centre for second-hand bookselling

RIDING ANTICLOCKWISE

After Knighton, the only places for food along the route are the general store and the inn at Beguildy. The store is closed on Wednesday and Saturday afternoons and all day Sunday, and the pub is closed on Mondays and every afternoon from 2pm until 6.00pm.

STAGE 11
Hay-on-Wye to Chepstow

Start	Hay-on-Wye, below Hay Castle (SO 231 423)
Finish	Chepstow Railway Station (ST 537 937)
Distance	51 miles (82km)
Ascent	1300m
Time	8–9hr
OS Maps	OS Landranger 171, 162 and 161
Refreshments	There are a few pubs in the villages along the way. However, many do not open during the day, so you can only rely on Abergavenny or Usk for refreshments
Accommodation	Plenty of accommodation of all types in towns, including hostels at Pantygelli near Abergavenny and Chepstow

Immediately after leaving Hay-on-Wye, the route slowly climbs up through the Gospel Pass providing breath-taking views northwards into central Wales and the English Marches. This is followed by a long descent through the delightful Vale of Ewyas, where there are plenty of antiquities to visit in the pleasant market town of Abergavenny. The next section through Usk is fairly easy, but there is a short, sharp climb at Pen-y-cae-mawr that leads up to the ancient woodlands of Wentwood. The route then runs gently downhill all the way to Chepstow with some fine views out across the Bristol Channel.

Ride along Castle Street and Church Street to the edge of the town centre and then turn sharp left into Forest Road to join NCN 42, which this stage follows all the way to Chepstow. There is an excellent cycle shop and café on a small industrial estate as you leave the town, where you could top up energy levels ready for 5 miles of climbing at a steady 5% gradient to the top of the **Gospel Pass**, which at 549m (1,801 ft) above sea level is the highest road pass in Wales.

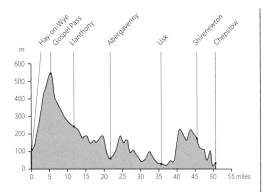

Gospel Pass (Bwlch yr Efengyl), which squeezes between the summits of Lord Hereford's Knob (690m) to the west and Hay Bluff (677m) to the east, is said to get its name from 12th-century crusaders who travelled this way – a plausible explanation as Llanthony Priory is just a few miles away down the Vale of Ewyas. What no one knows, though, is how Lord Hereford's Knob got its name.

Wild ponies on the slopes below the Gospel Pass

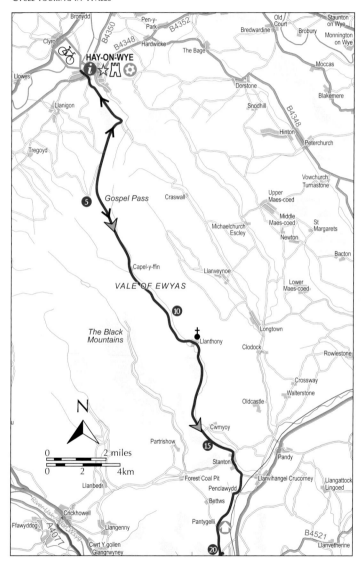

However, what really matters is the view you get from the col to the north. It runs all the way from the Brecon Beacons in the west around to the Cambrian Mountains in the north and seems to go on endlessly across the rolling Herefordshire countryside to Shropshire and beyond.

Once you are over the top, the next 15 miles down the **Vale of Ewyas** are predominantly downhill, but there are plenty of reasons to stop along the way. First comes Capel-y-ffin (8/43 miles), a tiny 18th-century chapel dedicated to St Mary, which has a twisted tower. ▶

There is more ecclesiastical interest 3 miles further on at **Llanthony** (11/40 miles), where the ruins of an early 12th-century Augustinian priory are located.

Its graveyard contains a headstone engraved by the sculptor, designer and typographer Eric Gill (1882–1940), who during the 1920s lived at nearby Capel-y-ffin Monastery, now a private residence.

The deposed Edward II stayed at **Llanthony Priory** on 4 April 1327 on his way to Berkeley Castle, where he is assumed to have been brutally murdered. The priory was once one of the most important medieval buildings in Wales, but its fortunes were already in decline before the Dissolution of the Monasteries. Its infirmary was converted into St David's Church, and other buildings were turned into a private house and subsequently a hotel.

Beyond Llanthony the valley is steeply banked and the road runs through a continual tunnel of hazel, oak and ash, so views are few and far between. However, you soon catch a glimpse of the village of **Cwmyoy** across the valley and it is worth making a detour to visit.

The largely 13th-century **Church of St Martin** at Cwmyoy, tucked into the wooded slopes of Hatterrall Hill on the opposite bank of Afon Honddu, is reputed to be the most crooked church in Great Britain. The local geology consists of Old Red Sandstone lying over marl, and over the centuries, slippage and subsidence have caused the tower and chancel to move in opposite directions,

Map continues on page 144

The 13th-century Church of St Martin, reputed to be the most crooked church in Great Britain, tucked into the wooded hillside at Cwmyoy

twisting the entire structure. You can ride a loop through the village by turning left as soon as you see its name on a signpost, rejoining the route a mile further on.

Just before Stanton (16/35 miles) is an old, stone-built pub complete with flagged floor and low beams. Unfortunately, like many rural pubs, it has limited opening hours during the week. Turn right a mile further on and right again in Pen-y-clawdd (18/33 miles) towards Abergavenny. There is a short climb around the south-eastern flanks of Sugar Loaf, but once past **Pantygelli** (19/32miles) it is downhill all the way to **Abergavenny** (22/29 miles).

Shortcut via Llantilio Pertholey
There is a shortcut around Abergavenny that saves just 2 miles. Turn left at a marker post a mile south of Panytgelli (SO 304 166) and follow this lane around to the right. Cross the Hereford Road and ride though **Llantilio Pertholey** and the tunnels under the A465 and the railway. Cross the B4521, ignoring route markers for NCN

46, and continue until you meet a prominent fingerpost.
Turn left to rejoin NCN 42 to Usk.

Turn left on to a shared-use path opposite the sports
field on the Old Hereford Road and then right along
Park Crescent at its end. Turn left into Penyfal Road by
the Labour Club and immediately left again into Skirrid
Road. Turn right into Park Avenue, then at its end by
the car park use the pelican crossing to cross Penyfal
Road into King Street. Turn right along Lion Street, then
dismount and turn left into the partly pedestrianized
Frogmore Street, then right into Nevill Street. Turn left by
the hotel at its end and ride along **Castle Street**, around

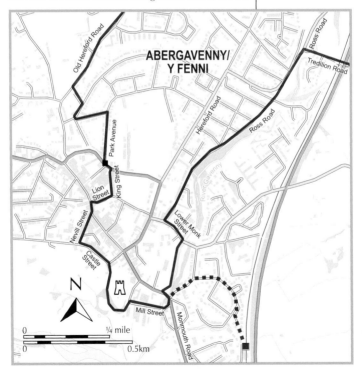

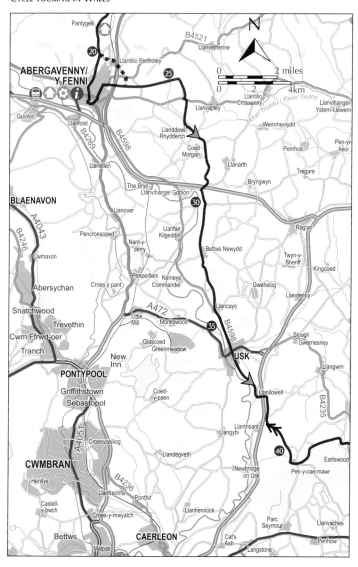

the ruins of the castle and into Mill Street. At its end turn left along the shared-use path along the busy Monmouth Road, then right through the little park once across the River Gavenny. Turn left at the end of the park and ride along Lower Monk Street, then turn right into Ross Road with the river below on the right. After three-quarters of a mile turn right into **Tredillon Road** and ride through the tunnels under the A465 and the railway and out into the country. This serpentine route is waymarked throughout. However, it is remarkably easy to become disorientated. So you can just head into the town centre to browse the shops and enjoy coffee and cake, and then find your way to Ross Road, which runs parallel with the A40 to the east of the town centre.

ABERGAVENNY

Abergavenny became an important centre both for the Romans and the Normans due to its location at the confluence of the River Gavenny and the River Usk. The town was granted the right to hold two weekly markets and three annual fairs in the 13th century and that tradition continues today, with local produce, crafts and antiques for sale in the busy Market Hall on most days. The annual Abergavenny Food Festival reinforces the town's reputation as a mecca for foodies, and you will find plenty of tempting gastro pubs, cafés and restaurants. In recent years the town has hosted the Abergavenny Festival of Cycling with an evening criterium for the professionals, a sportif and a number of events for leisure cyclists. For details see www.abergavennyfestivalofcycling.co.uk

Follow signs for NCN 46 past the prominent marker post by the gates to Tredilion Park, an early 18th-century mansion tucked teasingly out of sight in the trees, and follow this narrow lane for 2 miles. Turn left along the B4233 for a hundred metres then turn right alongside a white cottage. The road drops down to cross Pant Brook before climbing up through **Llanddewi Rhydderch** (27/24). After a mile turn right towards Coed Morgan, a tiny hamlet that is just off route to the right. It is a quiet lane running between low hedges that give good views

Map continues on page 147

west to the hills on the opposite bank of the River Usk and east towards the rolling Herefordshire countryside. Turn left at a marker post on a bend near Lower Coed Morgan Farm and follow this road for 1½ miles, crossing over the M40 to meet a junction devoid of direction signs other than one that points back to where you came from. Turn left and then half a mile later turn right towards **Bettws Newydd** in front of the late eighteenth-century Gothic gatehouse of Clytha Park, a 19th-century neoclassical country house hidden in the woods.

Since its restoration, the 19th-century Llancayo Windmill is available for self-catering holidays.

Pass through Bettws Newydd (32/19 miles), which is a pretty village although there is little reason to stop unless the pub is open. Two miles further on at Llancayo (34/17 miles) turn left and follow the B4598 into **Usk** (36/15 miles). ◀

In recent years **Usk** has achieved considerable success in Britain in Bloom competitions, with Her Majesty's Prison Usk, which today finds itself in a very suburban setting on the right as you enter the town, contributing to the display. With a number of pubs, restaurants, antique shops, a fine bridge and the remains of a 12th-century castle, Usk really ought to be more popular as a tourist destination. But perhaps visitors are deterred by the volume of traffic that passes through the centre on its way to and from the more industrial towns to the west.

Unless you are stopping to explore, turn right then quickly left through the traffic-free Maryport Street, heading southwards with the River Usk to the west. The route is easy going up until Llanllowell (38/13 miles), but shortly after passing under the busy A449, there is a 1 ½-mile (2.5km) climb at **Pen-y-cae-mawr**, with an average gradient of 8%. If you stop at the top by Pen-y-cae-mawr Chapel (42/9 miles) you get a wonderful view of the Black Mountains and the rolling Herefordshire countryside to the north.

After a hundred metres, turn left and ride along the quiet lanes around Wentwood, which is the largest

Looking towards the Black Mountains from Pen-y-cae-mawr Chapel

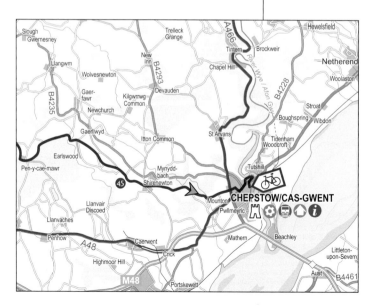

Wentwood provided oak for the British Navy's man-o'-war warships during the Napoleonic Wars in the early 19th century.

ancient woodland in Wales despite being a mere fragment of a far larger ancient forest. ◄ After 2 miles of pleasant cycling, which is now predominantly downhill, turn right towards Shirenewton, still following signs for NCN 42. Turn right again towards Chepstow soon after passing through the scattered village of Earlswood, where you get some fine views of the Bristol Channel to the south. Then turn left alongside the pub in the centre of **Shirenewton** (46/5miles).

Three miles further on, NCN 42 is joined by NCN 4 for the final 3 miles into **Chepstow**. When you meet the Wye Valley Link Road, turn right and follow the shared-use path, crossing to the town side of the main road around the busy Highbeech roundabout. Follow signs left to join Maple Road and then Mathern Road, passing first the town's cemetery and then Chepstow Athletic Club. Turn right at the junction with Bulwark Road, then immediately left along Strongbow Road. Turn left along a shared-use path that leads to Wye Crescent to emerge in Hardwick Avenue. Turn right along Garden City Way, with remains of the old town walls to your right, crossing Mount Pleasant then following a narrow path to emerge next to the 13th-century Town Gate in High Street.

Make your way downhill along High Street, Middle Street and Bridge Street until you meet the Old Town Bridge across the River Wye, which forms the border between England and Wales. Follow the one-way system back around the town and across Mount Pleasant to reach the end of the stage at **Chepstow Station**.

RIDING ANTICLOCKWISE

Take a break or stock up on food in Abergavenny, as there are only a couple of pubs along the next 22 miles to Hay-on-Wye, and they may not be open during the day.

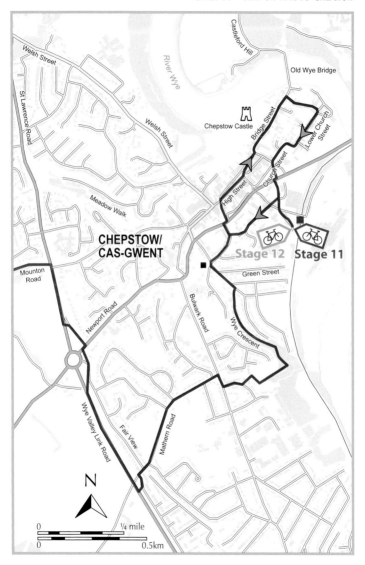

River Wye

Castleford Hill

Welsh Street

Old Wye Bridge

St Lawrence Road

Welsh Street

Chepstow Castle

Bridge Street

Lower Church Street

Church Street

High Street

Meadow Walk

**CHEPSTOW/
CAS-GWENT**

Stage 12 Stage 11

Green Street

Mounton Road

Newport Road

Bulwark Road

Wye Crescent

Wye Valley Link Road

Fair View

Mathern Road

N

| 0 | | ¼ mile |
| 0 | | 0.5km |

149

CHEPSTOW

Parked up on the English side of the Old Wye Bridge in Chepstow

Chepstow gets its name from the Old English *chepe stowe*, meaning a market place or trading place, and during the Middle Ages it was a major centre for importing wine from Europe and exporting timber from nearby woodlands. As the larger ports of Cardiff, Swansea and Bristol became more prominent in the early 19th century, Chepstow's importance diminished.

However, its picturesque location at the mouth of the River Wye meant trade was replaced with tourism, which remains an important part of the town's economy today. Old Wye Bridge is an elegant iron structure cast by John Rastrick of Bridgnorth in 1816. Chepstow Castle, which is the southernmost of a chain of border castles, was built by the Normans soon after their victory at the Battle of Hastings in 1066.

On 16 November 1854, the Victorian traveller George Borrow ended his journey through Wales at Chepstow by ordering the best dinner and a bottle of port at the principal hotel, to while away the hours before catching a late train to London. We have just 36 miles to go before we finish our journey around Wales.

STAGE 12
Chepstow to Cardiff

Start	Chepstow Railway Station (ST 537 937)
Finish	Cardiff Central Railway Station (ST 184 759)
Distance	36 miles (58km)
Ascent	200m
Time	4–5hr
OS maps	OS Landranger 171 and 170
Refreshments	The only food stops before Cardiff are the cafés, pubs and shops in Caldicot, Redwick and Newport, although you will have to temporarily leave the route to find them
Accommodation	No hostels until you reach Cardiff, but plenty of other choices in the main centres

This is an easy stage that crosses first the Caldicot Levels and then, after passing through the industrial outskirts of Newport, the Wentloog Levels. Enjoy the wide open spaces and big skies as the final 5-mile stretch is entirely urban. However, the route makes extensive use of Cardiff's network of shared-use paths and recommended cycle routes to make it as traffic free as possible.

Follow NCN 42 out of the town, reversing the final 2 miles of Stage 11. At the mini roundabout at the end of Mounton Road, bear left and follow NCN 4 along this wooded lane. Just before the busy A48, turn right and follow NCN 4 alongside the M48 motorway at first, then through **Caerwent** (7/29 miles), **Caldicot** (9/27 miles) and

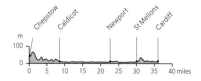

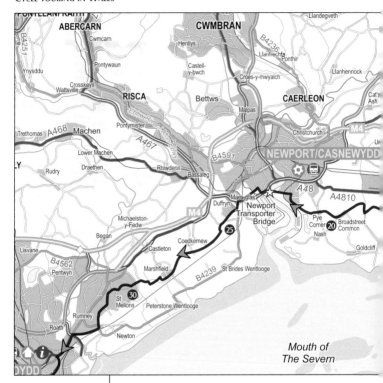

Map continues
on page 156

The Romans started
reclaiming land
here but most of
the reen system
dates from medieval
times and later.

over the M4 to join a gravel track. Enjoy the next 20 miles across the Caldicot and Wentloog Levels (low-lying estuarine alluvial wetland drained by dykes known locally as 'reens') because, unless you are heading into a gale, it is about as easy as cycling ever gets.

The first few miles immediately after crossing the M4 are on traffic-free tracks, although they are somewhat gravely, while the rest are on quiet roads. ◄ Keep following NCN 4 first through Undy (14/22 miles) and then **Redwick** (16/20 miles). On a warm day the only sound will be the low drone of flying insects and the sound of cattle stirring in the shade of the huge willow trees along the route.

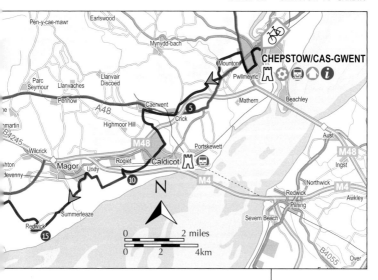

A mark on the south porch of the **Church of St Thomas the Apostle** in Redwick indicates the height to which floodwater rose on 30 January 1607. Recent geological analysis found an 8-inch-thick layer composed of sand, shells and stones within an otherwise homogenous deposit of mud, indicating a massive surge of water on the scale of a tsunami. Research into parish records on either side of the Bristol Channel also suggests that more than 2000 people were drowned in coastal villages, and entire buildings were swept away.

When you reach the junction at **Pye Corner** (20/16 miles), cross by the offices of the Caldicot and Wentloog Levels Drainage Board, follow a cycle track for 1 mile and then at its end pick up a cycle path alongside Corporation Road, heading towards Newport (22/14 miles). As long as it is between Easter and the end of September, not a Monday or a Tuesday and you have coins to pay the toll, you may choose to turn left along Stephenson Street and

use **Newport Transporter Bridge** across the River Usk. Otherwise, continue further along Corporation Road and turn left along the shared-use path that runs alongside the busy A48 to cross the river. Turn left and ride down Usk Way on the eastern bank until you reach the transporter bridge. Then dismount and use the designated crossing to reach Watch House Parade and follow it around into Mendalgief Road before turning left along Docks Way.

The **Newport Transporter Bridge**, which is a Grade I listed structure, is one of just eight transporter bridges remaining in use in the world. A

more traditional bridge would have required long
approaches to attain sufficient height to allow
ships to pass below. After city councillors viewed
a transporter bridge at Rouen, built by the French
engineer Ferdinand Arnodin, who had patented
the idea in 1887, they commissioned him to build
one for Newport. It is said to be the finest of its
kind with towers that stand 645ft apart and rise
242ft above the road.

Continue following NCN 4 waymarkers around a
roundabout, over the railway, around a second roundabout and over the River Ebbw. Turn left along Lighthouse
Lane and then right into Duffryn Way and follow the signs
around to Pencarn Way where the route stops following
NCN 4, which heads inland to Caerphilly. Turn left into
Morsaig Avenue at the next roundabout and follow waymarkers for NCN 88 out through the residential estate to
the Wentloog Level. Follow the route alongside Pencoed
Reen and into the appropriately named **Marshfield** (28/8
miles). ▶ Turn right along Marshfield Road, then left
into Pentwyn Terrace and then take the path through to
Wellfield Road. Turn left at the next junction, left again
after the bend and ride through the technology park,
where roads are named after programming languages, to
meet Cypress Drive, which at peak times is a busy dual
carriageway.

Turn left, cross at the lights and follow the
shared-use path alongside Faendre Reen and under
Willowbrook Drive. When you emerge on Crickhowell
Road, follow the path across the roundabout into
Brockhampton Road. Turn right just before the skate
park and cross the recreation ground in **St Mellons**.
Then cross Willowbrook Drive to Brookfield Drive and
follow the shared-use path through to **Greenway Road**.
Turn left and then after 1 mile cross Wentloog Road and
follow New Road for 1 mile. Turn left on to a shared-use
path by Rumney Pottery and follow it for 1 mile along-
side the busy Newport Road, before turning left at The
Royal Oak pub into **Beresford Street**. Take the second

Until NCN 88 is
extended beyond
Marshfield into
central Cardiff, the
remainder of this
stage through St
Mellons into Cardiff
city centre follows
local shared-use
paths and quieter
backstreets.

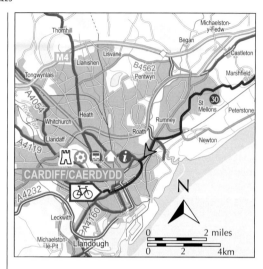

turn on the right after passing over the railway and ride along Carlisle Street and then Sanquhar Street. At its end, cross and turn left along the shared-use path and follow it around into **Tyndall Street**. Once over the railway, use the designated crossing if you are heading for the YHA Cardiff. Otherwise, carry on to Cardiff Central Station where this stage ends.

RIDING ANTICLOCKWISE

Finding one's way out of Cardiff can be confusing, especially if you have to concentrate hard just to stay safe in busy traffic. If you have a satnav for your bike then downloading the GPX track for the route will certainly help, (see www.cicerone.co.uk/988/GPX). Otherwise, study the detailed city map prior to setting out, and perhaps consider making your own route directions to help you identify the turns at least until you reach the shared-use path on Greenwood Road.

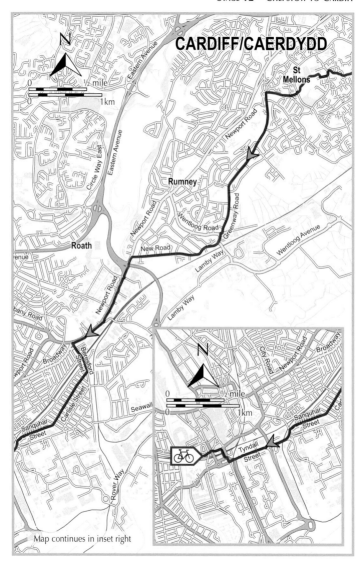

CARDIFF/CAERDYDD

St Mellons

Rumney

Roath

Map continues in inset right

THE SCOTTISH CONNECTION

Having arrived in Cardiff where being Welsh is celebrated in the arts, sport and everyday life, it's perhaps safe to suggest that none of this would have happened without one particular Scottish family that the Welsh themselves still hold dear to their hearts. For centuries the Earls of Bute had lived quietly on the island in the Firth of Clyde from which they took their title. All that changed in 1766 when the 4th Earl, and 1st Marquess, married the Honourable Charlotte Jane Windsor, who brought Cardiff Castle and large ancestral estates in South Wales into the family.

In 1801 Cardiff had a population of 1870, making it only the twenty-fifth largest town in Wales, well behind Merthyr Tydfil and Swansea. John Crichton-Stuart (1793–1848), the 2nd Marquess of Bute, soon changed its fortunes when he exploited its mineral reserves and developed the docks and transport connections. Cardiff soon became the main port for exports of coal and iron from the Valleys, and the city's population grew at a rate of nearly 80% per decade between 1840 and 1870. The 2nd Marquess's investments paid off handsomely, and he would later be known as 'the creator of modern Cardiff'. By the 1881 census, Cardiff had become the largest town in Wales. It became a city in 1905 and the capital in 1955.

His son, the 3rd Marquess of Bute (1847–1900), gained an inheritance that reportedly made him the richest man in the world. During his relatively short life he used his wealth to pursue his passions, which included medievalism and architecture, renovating and expanding both Cardiff Castle and Castell Coch, which are two of the finest examples of the late Victorian era Gothic Revival. The Marquess's patronage was also extensive and there is a park and many streets named after the family, showing just how highly esteemed the name Bute is in the city.

CROSS ROUTES

Parked up by the Sustrans pillar at the col between Foel Fadian and Bryn Y Fedwen on the mountain road between Llanidloes and Machynlleth (Cross route 3)

CROSS ROUTE 1
Wrexham to Bangor

Start	Wrexham General Railway Station (SJ 329 508)
Finish	Bangor Railway Station (SH 576 716)
Distance	73 miles (117km)
Ascent	1800m
Time	11–12hr
OS maps	OS Landranger 117, 125,116 and 115
Refreshments	Plenty of choice in the main towns along the way
Accommodation	Lots of accommodation of all types in all the main centres, including hostels in Llangollen, Cefn-brith, Betws-y-Coed, Capel Curig, Ogwen Cottage and Bethesda

This route visits all the main centres along the A5, but sticks to the quieter roads that run parallel to it for all but 5 miles through the Ogwen Valley where there are no alternatives available. Although you are never very far from the A5, it is a remarkably peaceful route with some wonderful scenery, especially through the Ogwen Pass where you are surrounded by some of the highest summits in Wales. Combined with Stages 7 and 8, it makes a wonderful short tour that could easily be ridden over a long weekend.

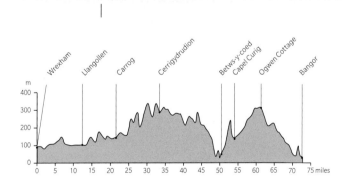

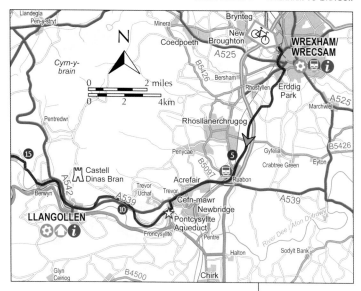

Cross route 1 begins by following the first 7 miles of Stage 9 (Wrexham to Acrefair), which is described again here. Head along Regents Street towards the town centre and then turn right on to the inner ring road at the traffic lights, following signs for Whitchurch. After 1 mile turn right off the tree-lined Fairy Road into Erddig Road and ride into Erddig Park. Pass Erddig Hall and bear right, taking the exit route to the right of the giant conifers.

Map continues on page 163

Turn left at the gatehouse and follow the blue cycle route markers along Hafod Road and New Hall Road to **Ruabon** (5/45 miles). Turn left along the High Street and then just after passing through the village centre, turn right into Wynnstay Gardens and follow a shared-use path alongside the railway. Turn right along the A539, soon picking up another shared-use path that leads across the main road and into the residential estate opposite. Ride along Hampden Way and Oak Road and then rejoin the main road. Ride downhill through **Acrefair** (7/44 miles).

Castell Dinas Brân was probably built in the 1260s by Gruffydd II ap Madog, a supporter of Llywelyn ap Gruffudd, the last sovereign Prince of Wales before its conquest by Edward I.

From Acrefair continue along the main road to Trevor (8/65 miles). Turn left down Station Road past the Grade II listed Bryn Seion Chapel, which is now a busy café, and cycle around the corner. Turn right opposite the entrance to **Pontcysyllte Aqueduct** and Trevor Basin and follow NCN 85 along the Llangollen Canal.

Although you are riding beneath trees for much of the time, you do get a glimpse of Castel Dinas Brân on one straight section by the hotel at Trevor Uchaf. ◀ As you approach **Llangollen** (12/61 miles), the towpath can be busy with walkers and dogs, so comply with the signs to dismount and walk until you are past this section.

Heading along the north bank of the River Dee between Llangollen and Carrog

There is plenty to look at as the **Llangollen Heritage Railway** runs parallel to the canal, and the permanent marquees of the **Llangollen International Musical Eisteddfod** are just below the towpath. This festival takes place every year during the second week of July and has hosted performers as diverse as the late Luciano Pavarotti, the Red Army Ensemble and the boy band, McFly.

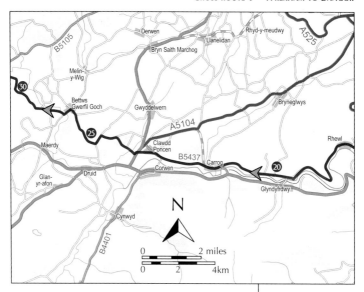

Leave the towpath at bridge 48AW, cross over the canal and then turn left along the B5103 and ride past Horseshoe Falls, where there are public toilets, and then past Llantysilio Church. Continue through **Rhewl** (16/57 miles) and Carrog (21/52 miles) with the River Dee meandering down in the valley on your left and the restored track of the Llangollen Railway and the busy A5 on the opposite bank.

Map continues on page 164

Turn left into Ffordd Ty Cerrig 500 metres after passing the turn for **Corwen** (24 miles) ▶ After 900 metres, turn left along the A494 and then immediately right into an unsigned side road. Climb steadily for 1½ miles and then turn left shortly after passing a white farmhouse with a fine stone barn. Turn left 200 metres further on at the next junction. Then after 600 metres, turn sharply right towards Bettws Gwerfil Goch. Turn left 2 miles further on and descend into **Bettws Gwerfil Goch** (28/45 miles). In the centre of the village, turn left towards Maerdy and then right just after crossing Afon Alwen. Follow this narrow

Best known for its connections with Wales's last unofficial king, Owain Glyndŵr, Corwen is a good place for a break as there is nothing for the next 10 miles.

163

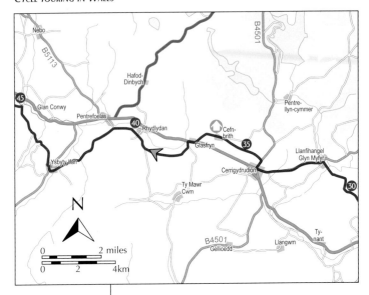

Map continues
on page 167

lane for 3 miles into **Llanfihangel Glyn Myfyr** (32/41 miles), taking care when crossing the cattle grids. Turn left along the B5105 and ride up and over to Cerrigydrudion (34/39 miles). Turn right towards Llyn Brenig and then quickly left towards Cefn-brith. Follow this road through Cefn-brith (36/37 miles) and down to meet the A5.

Turn right, ride or walk for 300 metres through **Glasfryn** and then turn left opposite the pottery. Turn right after crossing Afon Merddwr and ride along what becomes a concrete road, passing through two farmyards and a couple of gates. Turn right after 1 mile and ride down to the crossroads half a mile further on. Ignore the 'No Through Road sign', which seems to be there to prevent cars getting stuck on the grassy strip that runs down the middle of this little lane, and ride down to the junction by Capel Bethel. Turn left and after 900 metres turn left again towards **Ysbyty Ifan** (44/29 miles).

Go straight over at the crossroads in the middle of this interesting village and then 2 miles further on, where

YSBYTY IFAN

Ysbyty Ifan (the hospital of St John) became important after the Knights of St John established a hospital here at the end of the 12th century. Its purpose was to provide care and shelter for pilgrims travelling between religious sites in North Wales and to act as a retreat for members of their own order. During the 15th century the Red Bandits of Mawddwy, a band of red-haired thieves and highwaymen, used Ysbyty Ifan as a hideout, taking advantage of the Knights' privilege of sanctuary.

The hospital was abolished in 1540 during the Dissolution of the Monasteries, and the village church was built on its site; it is thought that John Morris, who lived in Bryn Gwyn (white hill), a farmhouse in the village that is now sadly derelict, may have worshipped here. In the first half of the 17th century, his daughter Ellen emigrated to Pennsylvania where she met and married Cadwaladr Evans who came from Bala not far from her family home. Their granddaughter Nancy was the mother of Abraham Lincoln who as President of the United States occupied the White House from 1861–1865.

Taking in the view above Ysbyty Ifan

the road drops sharply down towards the A5, turn left and ride along the undulating hillside. Take care as you drop down to meet the **B4406**. Cross into the narrow lane opposite and ride through the woodland to meet the A470. Turn right towards Betws-y-Coed. Then after 500 metres, turn left before Pont-yr-Afanc, the Grade II listed bridge that carries the A470 over the River Conwy, and follow the road into **Betws-y-Coed** (51/22 miles).

Although only just within the Snowdonia National Park, **Betws-y-Coed** sits in an attractive setting on the old coach road between London and Ireland, which meant it was always going to be a hot spot for travel and eventually tourism. When George Borrow passed through in the autumn of 1854, he delighted at the magnificent scenery and wrote, 'I was now amidst stupendous hills, whose paps, peaks and pinnacles seem to rise to the very heaven... Coming to the bottom of the pass I crossed over an ancient bridge (presumably Pont-yr-Afanc) and passing through a small town found

Passing a clump of wild garlic on the way to Betws-y-Coed

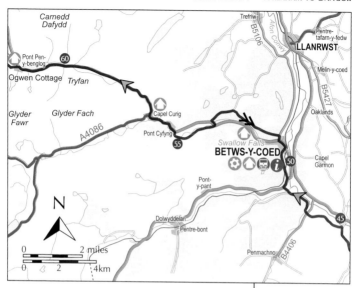

myself in a beautiful valley with majestic hills on
either side.'

Map continues
on page 168

The village boomed once the railway arrived
in 1868, and its easy access from the east has
helped the village establish itself as the gateway
to Snowdonia, with attractive shops and a wide
choice of places to eat and stay over.

Turn left and ride, or perhaps walk, through the busy
centre of the village. Turn right towards Trefriw and then
immediately left into Forest Road once over the bridge
across Afon Llugwy. Climb up through the trees, perhaps
dismounting and pushing up the short steep section and
up the ramp at the top where the road turns sharply right
and left between tidy stone walls. Turn left and enjoy a
wonderful descent on a super-smooth road to rejoin the
A5 by Ty Hyll (the Ugly House). Cross the bridge, turn
right and cycle along this quiet and almost entirely flat
lane to rejoin the A5 in **Capel Curig** (56/17 miles). Turn

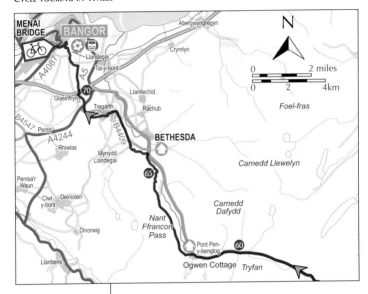

left and ride through Capel Curig, where there is an excellent outdoor café, a pub and a number of hotels.

If you are riding on beefy touring tyres, you could follow the old track that starts near the public conveniences and rejoin the A5 at the eastern end of Llyn Ogwen after 4 miles of traffic-free cycling. Otherwise, continue along the A5, which is thankfully broad and fairly straight, and enjoy the magnificent scenery with **Tryfan** and the Glyderau on your left and Pen yr Ole Wen and the Carneddau on your right. Borrow walked along this road but failed to be impressed, calling it 'a bleak moor, extending for a long way amidst wild sterile hills'. Somewhere along the valley, he met 'two wretched and sickly looking children' who parents made their living from producing wire-work for binding the tops of slate fences, which can still be seen in the area.

Turn left at **Ogwen Cottage** and follow NCN 82, or Lôn Las Ogwen as it is labelled locally, down the **Nant Ffrancon Pass** towards Bethesda (67/6 miles),

A local hill farmer and his dogs in the Nant Ffrancon Pass

SNOWDONIA NATIONAL PARK

The Snowdonia National Park, the first of the three national parks in Wales, covers 823 square miles (2130km²) in area and has 37 miles (60km) of coastline. The park includes all of the 15 Welsh summits over 3000ft. Starting with the distinctively pyramidal Tryfan (3011ft/918m) and moving around the Ogwen Valley in a clockwise direction, these include Glyder Fach (3261ft/994m), Glyder Fawr (3284ft/1001m), Y Garn (3107ft/947m) and Elidir Fawr (3031ft/924m) to the south of the A5 and Yr Elen (3156ft/962 m), Pen yr Ole Wen (3209ft/978m), Carnedd Dafydd (3425ft/1044m) and Carnedd Llewelyn (3491ft/1064m) to the north with Yr Elen (3156ft/962m) coming into view once past Ogwen Corner.

The dark cliffs of Cwm Idwal behind Ogwen Cottage provide shelter for rare plants that are the most southerly remnants of the Arctic and Alpine flora in Britain. These include the Snowdon lily (*Lloydia serotina*), which is only found at this spot in the UK, and other Alpine species, including the purple saxifrage (*Saxifraga oppositifolia*), tufted saxifrage (*Saxifraga cespitosa*), Alpine meadow rue (*Thalictrum alpinum*) and mountain sorrel (*Oxyria digyna*). Sheep are now excluded from the area to allow the native plants to flourish, and it is strictly managed as a National Nature Reserve.

Penrhyn Quarry, above Bethesda, was once the largest slate quarry in the world, employing around 3000 men. Today, it remains the largest quarry in Britain, although its workforce is now nearer 200.

passing piles of slate spoil that form the surface of the track. ◄ Eventually NCN 82 joins the B4409 for 1½ miles. But on the outskirts of **Tregarth** (69/4 miles), turn right along Maes Ogwen and follow signs for NCN 82 on to a reclaimed railway line that was built to carry slate down to the quay at Port Penrhyn. It is a superb shared-use path that includes a section of ravine, the 275m-long Tregarth Tunnel and a viaduct over Afon Ogwen.

Follow it for 2 miles along the bank of Afon Cegin until reaching the junction with NCN 5. If you are heading to Conwy, turn right here and then follow NCN 5. Otherwise, leave NCN 82 and turn left along Lon Cefn Ty. Use the footbridge to cross the ford and then after 500 metres turn right and then right again after another 200 metres and ride into **Bangor**. Bangor is the oldest city in Wales, having used the title by ancient prescriptive right until the Queen officially granted it city status in 1974. Turn left along High Street and follow signs for the railway station where this route ends.

RIDING WEST TO EAST

If you are happy riding in traffic and the road is not too busy, ignore the detour that starts at the Ugly House and ride along the A5 to Betws-y-Coed. It is mostly downhill so it will soon be over.

CROSS ROUTE 2
Barmouth to Chirk

Start	Barmouth Railway Station (SH 612 158)
Finish	Chirk Railway Station (SJ 284 379)
Distance	72 miles (115km)
Ascent	2000m
Time	12–13 hr
OS maps	OS Landranger 124, 125, 126 and 117
Refreshments	The longest stretches without a café or pub are the 22-mile section between Dolgellau and Llanuwchllyn and the 12-mile stretch over the Berwyn Mountains
Accommodation	Mainly concentrated at Dolgellau (9 miles) and Bala (40 miles), both of which have a good section of all types of accommodation, including hostels

This is a challenging route that first crosses the empty hills above the Coed-y-Brenin Forest and then crosses the Berwyn Mountains, each time climbing up to 500m above sea level. If the weather is good, the views are exceptional. If you have wide tyres and are willing to tolerate a certain amount of discomfort, you can choose to follow NCN 82 through the gravelly fire roads in Coed-y-Brenin Forest rather than going through Abergeirw.

Turn right out of the station and then right again along Beach Road towards the seafront. Turn left along the promenade, following waymarkers for NCN 8 and ride around the Quay before turning right towards Dolgellau. Climb up Porkington Terrace for 350 metres, then follow NCN 8 through a gap in the wall and cross Barmouth Viaduct, which on a fine day gives excellent views up the Mawddach Estuary.

Swing left just after Morfa Mawddach Station and follow the Mawddach Trail for 7 miles to the outskirts of **Dolgellau** (9/64 miles). ▶ There are couple of gates and a few speed bumps to look out, but plenty of opportunity to enjoy the birdlife along the estuary, where warblers

The Mawddach Trail follows the route of the Cambrian Line (1867–1965), which ran across Wales from Barmouth to Ruabon via Bala.

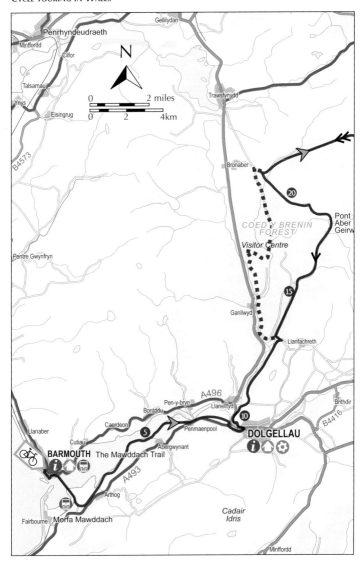

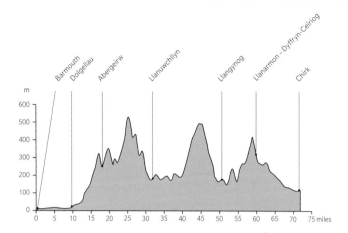

chatter away in the reeds and shelducks busily forage on the mudflats.

Up until the 19th century, when mechanical looms put an end to hand looms, weaving wool was an important activity in **Dolgellau**. So too was tanning, but that died out in the 1980s shortly after Dolgellau lost its administrative status as the county town of Merionethshire and became part of Gwynedd. However, its position at the foot of Cadair Idris, the second most popular mountain in Wales after Snowdon, means Dolgellau has a thriving economy based on tourism, although agriculture still plays a role with a popular farmers' market taking place on the third Sunday of every month.

Turn left where NCN 8 intersects with NCN 82, cross the footbridge over the A470 and then dismount and walk up the steep incline to the minor road that runs parallel. Turn left and follow NCN 82 towards Abergeirw along a quiet and surprisingly smooth road that runs along the hill-side above Afon Mawddach, with the ruins of 12th century Cymer Abbey down in the valley by the caravan site.

Map continues on page 175

Taking a break before the descent to Llanuwchllyn

Abergeirw, which consists of just nine properties strung out along this lonely road, was the last village in Wales to be supplied with mains electricity.

Two miles further on where the road turns away from the river to cross a tributary, turn right towards Abergeirw and climb steeply up through the trees. After 500 metres turn left and ride up to Capel Hermon where there is a welcome café 400 metres off route along the side road opposite the phone box. Continue climbing and then drop down to cross **Pont Abergeirw** (18/55 miles), which is the only landmark in the elusive village of Abergeirw whose name has appeared on road signs for the last 15 miles. ◄ Three miles further on, cross Afon Gain and turn right towards Llanuwchllyn.

Alternative route through Coed-y-Brenin Forest
If you wish to ride through Coed-y-Brenin, which is a busy centre for mountain biking with a bike shop and a café, keep following waymarkers for NCN 82. Ride up through the woods and around the visitor centre, where it is easy to lose track of waymarker signs. If in doubt, head up to the overflow car park and ride past The Foundry/Y Ffowndri to regain the trail, which is thankfully much more compacted and comfortable to ride on than the lower slopes before

the visitor centre. One mile after leaving the woods, stop following NCN 82 and turn right towards Llanuwchllyn by an isolated bus shelter, following blue signs for Regional Route 13. Ride downhill and turn left towards Llanuwchllyn to rejoin the route.

Climb steadily for 4 miles to an altitude of 530 metres, passing through a number of farm gates and the occasional farmyard. The only vegetation is heather, scrubby birch and a few conifers but most likely you will have the sharp ringing call of the stonechat or, in spring, the distinctive call of the cuckoo for company. If you look back down the valley on a clear day, you can see the Rhinogs, the range of hills that lie inland behind Harlech, which rise to 756m (2480ft) at their highest point.

Enjoy 5 miles of glorious descent alongside Arfon Lliw, taking care near the bottom where a gate, a couple of steep sections with gradients of 12% and 17% and a cattle grid come in rapid succession. Soon after passing

Map continues
on page 177

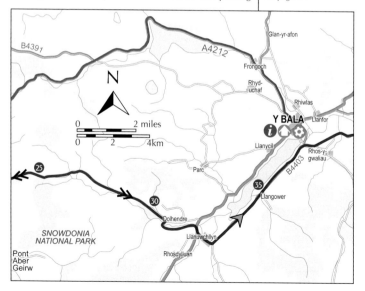

175

The Bala Lake Railway runs for 4.5 miles along the eastern shore of the lake from Llanuwchllyn to Bala along the track of the former line between Barmouth and Ruabon.

through the last gate, turn right at a junction by a public telephone box in the hamlet of **Dolhendre** (31/42 miles) and follow signs for Regional Route 14 across Arfon Lliw. Turn right along the A494, then after just 250 metres, turn left along the B4403 towards Llangower. Ride through **Llanuwchllyn** (33/40 miles), where there is a community-run inn and shop, and then **Llangower** (35/37 miles), following the quiet road along the eastern shore of Llyn Tegid/Bala Lake. ◄ The town of Bala is one mile off route at the head of the lake.

> **Llyn Tegid** (the fair lake) is the largest natural body of water in Wales. It is a popular location for sailing, canoeing and angling as it has large populations of pike, perch, brown trout, roach and eel. Until recently it was also the only known location of the gwyniad, a freshwater white fish that is distantly related to the salmon. But over recent years declining water quality and the human introduction of the invasive and non-native ruffe have threatened the population and stocks have been moved to nearby Llyn Arenig Fawr as a conservation measure.

Follow the shared-use path around the top of the lake if you wish to visit Bala, where George Borrow enjoyed ale equal to the best he had ever drunk, 'rich, mellow, with scarcely any smack of hop in it, and though so pale and delicate to the eye nearly as strong as brandy'. If you have no desire to discover whether the town still provides such delights and want to continue, turn right along the **B4391** towards Llangynog. The first 3 miles along the Dee Valley are fairly easy going, but once the road starts to zig-zag through the trees, it all changes as the route starts to climb across the sparsely populated Berwyn Mountains, eventually reaching an altitude of 486m. The first mile of ascent, where the road winds through the trees, is by far the steepest and after that it is easier to suppress any discomfort by concentrating on the glorious views. At the top of the pass,

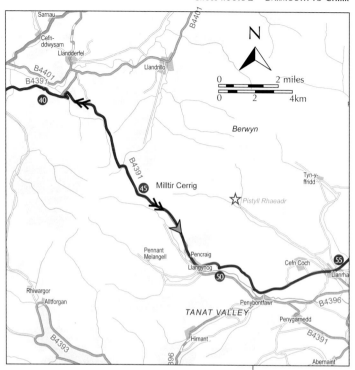

which is called **Milltir Cerrig** ('Mile of Stones' – pre-sumably referring to some long-lost waymarkers), a bri-dleway leads north-east for 4 miles to Cadair Berwyn, which at 832m is the highest summit in the range.

Once over the top keep a look out for the odd patch of loose gravel during the 5 miles of descent down the glorious Tanat Valley to **Llangynog** (48/25 miles). Turn left at an unsigned junction by the caravan park before the village centre and follow this quiet road around to the right. Continue along the hillside below Craig Rhiwarth and then after 3 miles, turn left by a bridge across Afon Tanat and ride to **Llanrhaeadr-ym-Mochant** (53/20 miles). ▸

Map continues on page 179

Ym-Mochant means 'in Mochant', which was an administrative district in the county of Powys during the medieval era.

George Borrow wrote he had never seen water falling so gracefully as at Pistyll Rhaeadr, which is 4 miles off route to the north-west of Llanrhaeadr-ym-Mochant

Pistyll Rhaeadr, which is 4 miles off route to the north-west of Llanrhaeadr-ym-Mochant, may not be the highest waterfall in Wales, but it can claim to be the prettiest. In his book, *Wild Wales*, the 19th-century travel writer George Borrow wrote that he had never seen water falling so gracefully. Follow the brown tourist signs up the dead end to the waterfall, where there is also a café.

Bear left by the public convenience in the village square, heading towards Llanarmon Dyffryn Ceiriog, which is abbreviated to Llanarmon DC on the road sign.

Then after 500 metres, turn off the main road, still following signs for Llanarmon DC, which now appears in
full. There is a short steep section just after crossing Afon
Iwrch, where it is best to dismount and walk, followed
by a gentler ascent around the eastern flanks of Mynydd
Mawr before an enjoyable descent to **Llanarmon Dyffryn
Ceiriog** (59/14 miles). ▶

The climbing is now all done and the remainder of
the route is downhill. Cross the bridge over Afon Ceiriog
and ride down the Ceiriog Valley, passing through the
hamlets of Tregeiriog (62/12 miles) and Pandy (64/9
miles). Rather than sticking to the B4500, turn left in **Glyn**

Despite its small size
Llanarmon DC has
two fine pubs, one
of which is listed as
one of the 30 cosiest
pubs in Britain by a
national newspaper.

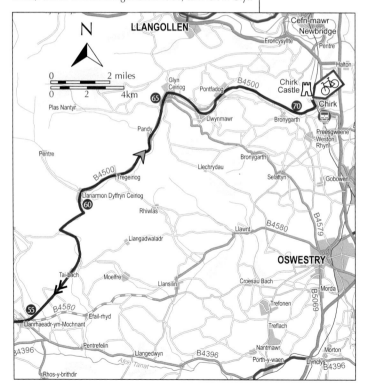

179

The Glyn Ceiriog Tramway Trust is currently working to reinstate a narrow-gauge railway that between 1873 and 1935 carried granite and slate from quarries around the head of valley down to Chirk.

Ceiriog (65/8 miles), taking the road between the village shop and war memorial, and then after 300 metres turn right by a timber-clad house to join the Ceiriog Cycle Route. ◀ This well-signed route, which has yet to be incorporated into the NCN, sticks to the quieter roads along the hillside either side of the B4500. Follow it to Dolywern, where it crosses the main road to join a quiet lane along the opposite bank of Afon Ceiriog. A mile further on, turn right and follow the B4500 through **Pontfadog** (69/4miles) to **Chirk**, abandoning the Ceiriog Cycle Route, which further on has some steep climbs that would be decidedly unwelcome so late in the route. Turn left at the mini roundabout and ride to the railway station where the route ends. Chirk was once a busy stop on the old coach route from London to Holyhead, as well as a bustling coal mining community, which employed 2000 colliers at its height until the last mine closed in 1968.

RIDING EAST TO WEST

Refuel in Llanrhaeadr-ym-Mochant for the climb through the Berwyn Mountains and in Bala for the climb through the high hills above the Coed-y-Brenin Forest, which rise to more than 500m above sea level.

CROSS ROUTE 3
Welshpool to Machynlleth

Start	Welshpool Railway Station (SJ 229 072)
Finish	Machynlleth Railway Station (SH 745 013)
Distance	54 miles (87km)
Ascent	1200m
Time	8–9hr
OS maps	OS Landranger 126, 136 and 135
Refreshments	Plenty of choice in the main towns, but little between Llanidloes and Machynlleth other than just off route at Staylittle and at Dylife
Accommodation	Lots of B&Bs and hotels in the towns, and there are hostels at Llanidloes and Dylife

This route first follows the River Severn upstream to the pleasant town of Llanidloes and then climbs gently up through the Hafren Forest and over the Cambrian Mountains, along what is known locally as 'the Mountain Road', to the wonderfully eclectic town of Machynlleth. Navigation is easy as the route follows NCN 81 to Llanidloes and then NCN 8 to Machynlleth. However, the first 14 miles along the Montgomery Canal to the outskirts of Newtown may not be waymarked, as the project to restore this lovely canal is not yet complete.

Leave the station and follow road signs for the town centre. Then half way along Seven Street, drop down to the Montgomery Canal just before the bridge by the Powysland Museum and follow the towpath past **Berriew** (5/49 miles). The canal is currently being restored and as yet there is only an isolated 17-mile run around Welshpool open for navigation, so you will have few narrowboats for company and will have to make do with a few swans or the occasional statuesque heron.

At Garthmyl (7/47 miles) the canal disappears underground through a conduit beneath the A483. To rejoin

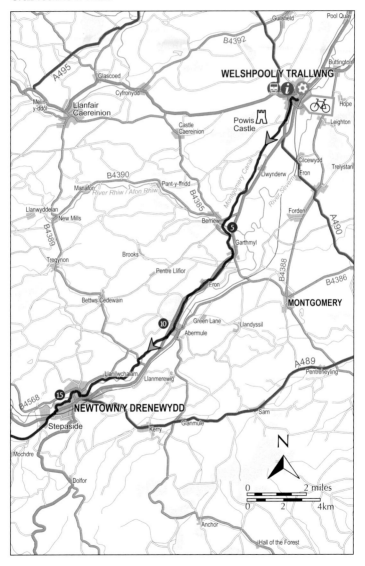

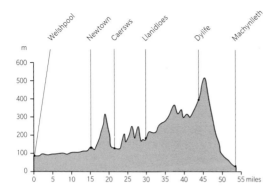

the towpath, turn left through the gate, cross the main road by the Nags Head Inn and then turn left towards Montgomery. The A483 has to be crossed twice before you reach **Abermule** (10/44 miles), but neither is quite as confusing as that at Garthmyl, which would undoubtedly benefit from waymarker signs.

As you approach **Newtown**, the path has the canal on one side and the River Severn on the other. The canal then becomes less distinct, first dwindling to an overgrown ditch before disappearing for good. The fact that the path passes under what is evidently a canal bridge suggests it is buried somewhere deep underground.

At the time of writing, the first waymarker sign for NCN 81 had appeared on the outskirts of Newtown (14/40 miles). As you approach the town centre, follow the blue waymarker signs for NCN 81 around into Cambrian Gardens and across the footbridge to the opposite bank of the River Severn. Follow the path along the riverbank, past one of the town's car parks and through a park to meet Park Road. Turn right and follow signs for NCN 81 across the mini roundabout and along Lon Cerddyn to the A489. Turn right and follow the shared-use path across the pedestrian crossing, through a tunnel under the railway and around the edge of the residential estate to **Mochdre Industrial Estate**. Turn left, keep to the

Map continues on page 186

NEWTOWN

Newtown, which is the largest town in Powys, dates back to the 13th century. It remained small until the 18th and 19th centuries when it became an important centre for flannel and wool, with the town's Cambrian Mills being the largest and most technically advanced woollen manufacturer in Wales until it was destroyed by fire in 1912.

In the middle of the 18th century local draper Pryce Pryce-Jones (1834–1920) exploited the opening of the railway in 1863 and improvements in the postal service to establish the UK's first large-scale mail order business. It supplied customers across the globe with locally made woollen goods, including what is considered to be the first ever sleeping bag, which Pryce-Jones patented in 1876 under the name of the Euklisia Rug. By 1880 he had more than 100,000 customers, including Queen Victoria, who knighted him in 1887. The Royal Welsh Warehouse that Pryce-Jones built in 1879 to house his thriving business stills stands next to the town's station.

Pryce-Jones will have undoubtedly known the textile mill owner and social reformer Robert Owen (1771–1858) who was born in Newtown. After learning the textile trade locally and later in Manchester, Owen famously took over a textile mill at New Lanark in Scotland, which he ran on philanthropic principles, introducing radical improvements in the living conditions, health and education of his employees. He repeated his utopian experiment at New Harmony in Indiana, USA, but returned to Newtown in later life and is buried in the graveyard of Newtown Parish Church. You can visit Newtown Textile Museum, the Robert Owen Museum and the WH Smith Museum, which traces the history of the retailer from its beginnings in London, in 1792, to the present day. All of the museums are located in the centre of town.

Stepaside occurs elsewhere as a place name and is thought to date from the Civil War when Cromwell's army reputedly asked people in its way to step aside.

shared-use path and take the second exit off the roundabout signed for Units A-B, 1–23.

Ride under the flyover, which carries a new ring road, and into Stepaside (17/37 miles). ◀ Turn right towards **Caersws** in the centre of the village and then after following this meandering lane for 4 miles, cross the A489 and the railway and ride into Caerwys (22/32 miles). Turn left towards Trefeglwys, ride past the railway station and then turn left immediately after crossing Afon Carno. After 1½ miles turn left towards Llandinam, then turn right at the

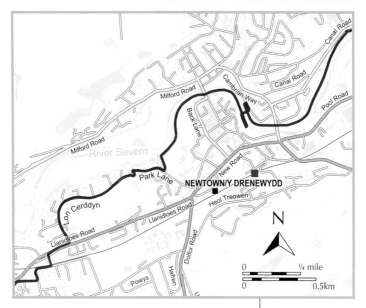

next junction, following signs for NCN 81. At the next junction, where a Presbyterian Chapel stands opposite a matching school that has been meticulously restored, turn right and climb up and over a little hill to meet the B4569. Turn left and ride into **Llanidloes** (30/24 miles).

The first town on the River Severn, **Llanidloes** was once an important centre for flannel. Before the 19th century it was a cottage industry and many of the three-storey houses in the town would have housed weaving lofts in the upper storey. Mechanization shifted production into mills, such as the one by the River Severn. The new technology was far from profitable and production dwindled, resulting in a local Chartist revolt in 1839. Its ringleaders were arrested, tried and sentenced to imprisonment or transportation. The last mill closed in 1913.

The half-timbered Old Market Hall in Llanidloes

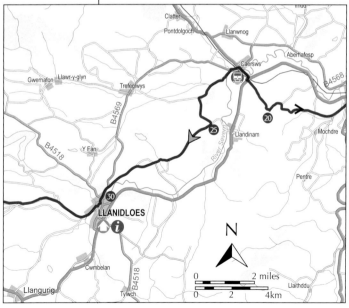

The half-timbered **Old Market Hall** was built around 1600 and is the only surviving building of this type in Wales. Assize courts were held in the upper hall during the 17th century, and John Wesley preached from a pulpit stone on the open ground floor in 1748. Today, Llanidloes looks like a traditional market town but still retains a reputation for radicalism and quirkiness, making it a popular retreat for those seeking an alternative lifestyle, much like neighbouring Machynlleth.

Turn right around the Old Market Hall, ride along Short Bridge Street and across the bridge over the River Severn, then bear left into Penygreen Road and follow this narrow road for the next 10 miles. It is gentle climbing initially with the River Severn down in the valley to your left. Then once within the boundaries of the **Hafren Forest** the road swings northwards away from the river close to its source on the lower slopes on nearby Plynlimon (752m/2467ft), which is the highest summit in Mid Wales.

The **Hafren Forest**, which covers around 15 square miles, consisted of pine and spruce when it was planted in 1937, but in recent decades native species have been introduced to create greater biodiversity and more varied habitats for wildlife. The seeds of the conifers attract flocks of crossbills that feed high up in the tree tops, and the newly planted areas make an ideal habitat for the nightjar. But the outstanding success in recent years has been a pair of ospreys successfully rearing young at a site on Llyn Clywedog, adjacent to the route.

Shortly after leaving the forest, turn left near Staylittle (41/13 miles), an isolated village with such patchy mobile coverage it is reputed to attract visitors looking for a digital detox. Ride along the B4518 for a mile, then turn left towards Machynlleth. After half a mile, there is a viewpoint into the V-shaped **Dylife**

Map continues on page 188

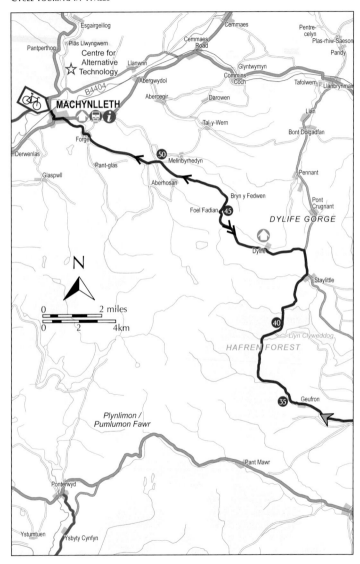

Looking down the Dylife Gorge

Gorge, which was formed as a U-shaped valley during the last ice age but which has been further eroded by the fast-flowing River Twymyn. ▶

Ride on through Dylife (14/25 miles), where lead was mined until the end of the 19th century, and climb gently for 3 miles up the south-west slopes of **Foel Fadian** (564m/1850ft), reaching an altitude of 512m on the col between the summit and Bryn y Fedwen.

> Along the road to the north-east of the summit of Foel Fadian is a memorial to the broadcaster **Wynford Vaughan-Thomas** (1908–1987) who was president and chairman of the Campaign for the Protection of Rural Wales between 1968 and 1975. Built from local slate, the memorial is in the form of a toposcope looking out over the rolling hills and mountains to the north, with Snowdon, Wales's highest peak, just visible on a clear day.

> After an enjoyable view comes 8 miles of downhill to Machynlleth. There are no junctions but take care as

The 40m-high Ffrwd Fawr waterfall is tucked out of sight at the bottom of the Dylife Gorge below the viewpoint.

The monument to Wynford Vaughan-Thomas high above the Dovey Valley near Machynlleth

you will meet farm traffic and possibly a golfer because the road passes through the town's course. At the end of the road, turn left into the centre of **Machynlleth**, then right at the clock tower and ride to the station where the route ends.

RIDING WEST TO EAST

Be prepared for the long climb out of Machynlleth, which is fairly gentle until the corners at the top where gradients exceed 10%.

CROSS ROUTE 4
Aberystwyth to Knighton

Start	Aberystwyth Railway Station (SN 585 815)
Finish	Knighton Railway Station (SO 291 724)
Distance	71 miles (114km)
Ascent	1800m
Time	11–12 hr
OS maps	OS Landranger 135, 136 and 137
Refreshments	There is a great cycle-friendly café that sells essential spares in Pont-rhyd-y-groes and plenty of places to eat or stock up on supplies in Rhayader – but little thereafter
Accommodation	Plenty of choice of all types of accommodation around Rhayader – but little before or after

This is a wonderful route that initially follows Lôn Ystwyth (NCN 81) gently up into hills along the course of an old railway track. Easy climbing then leads up across open moorland and down through the reservoirs in Elan Valley to Rhayader. From there the route follows NCN 825 through rolling hills to Knighton with hardly any flat. This makes the riding considerably more energy-sapping than the first half, so make sure to refuel or stay overnight in Rhayader.

Turn left out of the station and left into Park Avenue at the mini roundabout. After 200 metres turn right into Greenfield Street, opposite the retail park, and then at its end turn left along Riverside Terrace. Turn quickly right following signs for NCN 81, the Ystwyth Trail, along a shared-use path and cross the footbridge over Afon Rheidol. Follow the NCN 81 along Spring Gardens, across Penparcau Road and into Felin-y-Mor Road between Pendinas and the Irish Sea. ▶

Cross the A487 near **Llanfarian** and ride along the foot of the hill following the course of an old railway line along the bank of Afon Ystwyth. This railway track once

Plans to install a statue of the Duke of Wellington (1769–1852) at the top of the monument on Pendinas never came to fruition, and it is now conveniently said to represent a vertical cannon.

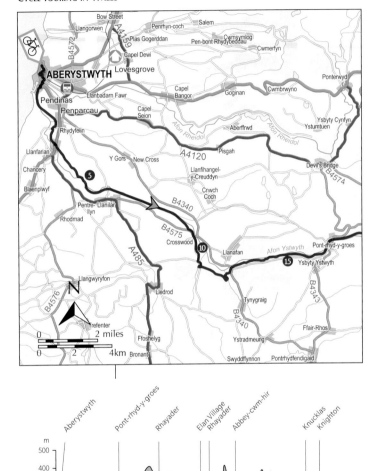

connected Aberystwyth with Carmarthen, and the surface is mostly good although there is a short stretch littered with stones where anyone on skinny tyres may want to dismount and walk. Inevitably, there are a few gates and a few short diversions along minor roads where the track has been built over.

After 9 miles cross the **B4575**, then follow NCN 81 markers up and along the hillside, passing through a couple of cuttings that show NCN 81 is once again following the course of the old railway track. Carefully descend a short stretch of path that drops quite steeply, cross the footbridge at the ford and then turn left along the B4340. Enjoy 400 metres of swooping descent and then turn right before the bridge and follow this minor road up through the wooded valley, with Afon Ystwyth down on your left. Turn left along the B4343 and ride through **Pont-rhyd-y-groes** (15/56 miles) where the café is a frequent destination for the local cycling club. ▶ When George Borrow passed through Pont-rhyd-y-groes on his way to the abbey at Strata Florida, he encountered a boisterous wedding party who jeered at the way he spoke Welsh

Parked up on the footbridge by the ford on Lôn Ystwyth

Map continues on page 194

The waterwheel in Pont-rhyd-y-groes was constructed to commemorate how important lead mining was in the area; it is driven by floodwater draining out of mines higher up the hillside.

193

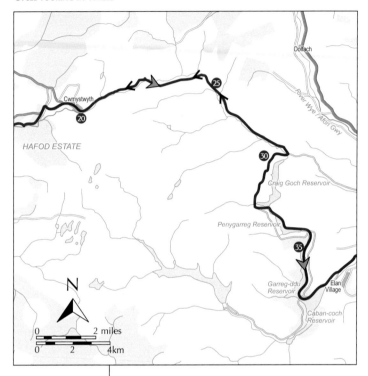

Map continues
on page 196

and then derided him even more loudly when he resorted to English.

Immediately after crossing Afon Ystwyth turn right by a gatehouse to join a gravelly track through the woods and parkland of the Hafod Estate, which George Borrow also visited while travelling through Mid Wales.

Thomas Johnes (1748–1816) inherited the 10,000-acre **Hafod Estate** from his father in 1780 and soon set about building a new lavishly decorated mansion in the then fashionable Gothic style and created a 'picturesque landscape' by planting 3 million trees to create over 1000 acres of forest. Johne's first mansion was destroyed by a fire in 1807, and a replacement he built was vacated by its last owner in 1946 and demolished in 1958. The estate is currently owned by Natural Resources Wales, which, in partnership with the Hafod Trust, manages conservation and restoration projects so the public can enjoy Johne's network of woodland walks.

At the end of the track through the estate, turn right along the B4574 towards Elan and ride through the scattered village of **Cwmystwyth** (19/52 miles) and up the valley, which is lined with the derelict buildings and spoil heaps from numerous lead mines that tunnel deep into the hillside. Climb steadily up to the moor where as long as there is no headwind to battle against, you can enjoy a gentle descent down to Pont ar Elan. Turn right towards the Elan Valley, still following signs for NCN 81, and enjoy some swooping bends down to Afon Elan before settling in to more undulating downhill alongside the first reservoir.

Cross the dam at the end of **Craig Goch Reservoir** and follow a gravel track gently downhill along the

The impressive dam holds back the water in Craig Goch Reservoir

eastern shores of Penygarreg Reservoir, Garreg-Ddu Reservoir and then Caban-Coch Reservoir to **Elan Village** (37/34 miles),

Elan Village was built in the Arts and Crafts style to house the workers and their families responsible for maintaining the reservoirs, dams and filtration systems constructed between 1892 and 1904 to supply water to Birmingham. No pumps are needed as the water pipes drop 52 metres (171ft) along the 73 miles (117km) from Elan to Birmingham. The gentle gradient of 1:2300 means the waters flows at less than 2 miles per hour (3.2km/h), taking 2–3 days to reach the storage reservoir to the south-west of the city.

Map continues
on page 198

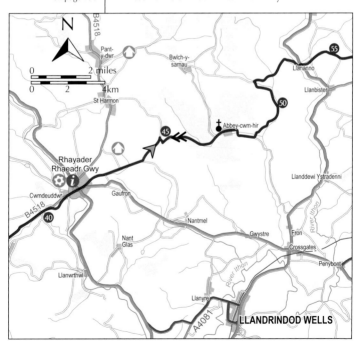

196

The shared-use path continues all the way into Rhayader. However, its popularity with young families may drive you out along the B4518 until it becomes less busy nearer the town. Rejoin it at its junction with NCN 8 and follow it through the woods and wildlife reserve. Pass through the elaborately carved gate, turn right and ride through **Cwmdauddwr**, across the bridge over the River Wye and into **Rhayader** (40/31 miles).

RHAYADER

Rhayader was once a stopping place for monks travelling between the abbeys of Strata Florida to the west and Abbey-cwm-hir to the north-east. Drovers also passed through, driving their livestock to markets in the Midlands. Perhaps this explains why the town has the highest concentration of pubs per head of population of any town in the UK, with one to every 173 people.

Today, Rhayader is an important centre for tourists visiting the impressive reservoirs and dams in the nearby Elan Valley, as well as those wanting to see red kite. There is a Red Kite Feeding Centre on the southern edge of the town where you can watch them at close quarters. However, these elegant birds are no longer rare and you may see them anywhere in central Wales, soaring on their curved wings and twisting their long forked tails to change direction.

War memorial clock tower dating from 1924 in the centre of Rhayader

Ride along West Street, past the town's war memorial and out along East Street, heading towards Leominster. Turn left towards Abbey-cwm-hir, now following NCN 825 all the way to Knighton. Four miles outside the town, bear right and climb steadily up Lan Goch (red bank). The ascent is just over half a mile at a gradient of 10%, but it seems infinitely harder. However, the fine views back across the Wye Valley and the likelihood of sighting red kite mean there plenty of excuses for a rest.

Once over the top the scenery changes from open hillsides to conifer plantations. What's more it is downhill all the way into **Abbey-cwm-hir** (47/24 miles), although there are still plenty of little hills along the remainder of

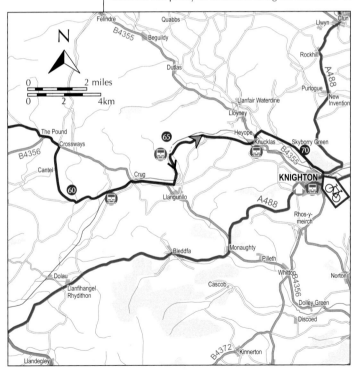

the route. ▶ A mile beyond the village, turn left at an unmarked junction and ride gently up the valley, briefly following Glyndŵr's Way. Ride through a farmyard, turn right and climb through a low gap in the hills before dropping down to **Llananno** (53/18 miles).

Turn left along the A483 towards Llandrindod Wells and then left by the public toilets. Climb up away from the main road, following signs for NCN 825 across a staggered junction, heading towards Llangunllo. Ride past a sheep farm, pass through two farm gates and climb up to a ridge, which gives distant views all around.

Turn right towards Llangunllo at the junction at the end of the ridge and left a mile further on in the tiny hamlet of **The Pound** (56/15 miles). Ride though Crossways, turn right towards Cantel and ride across Litttlehill Common and down into and back up out of Cantel. Turn left towards Llanbister at the top of the climb. Ride past Llanbister Road Station and then turn right towards Llangunllo at the next junction with the railway to your left. Turn left towards Knucklas a mile further on and left again after 400 metres heading for an unnamed station, which turns out to be **Llangunllo Railway Station**.

Keep following the road around the valley with the railway still to your left, and ride through **Heyope**, with its leaning church tower, to **Knucklas** (68/3 miles), where a 13-arch, castellated viaduct carries the railway over tributaries of the River Teme. Ride through the village, across the B4355 and over the bridge across the River Teme. Turn right towards Skyborry Green and follow this quiet lane for the final two miles to the end of the route at **Knighton Railway Station**.

Had it been completed the 12th-century Cistercian abbey at Abbey-cwm-hir would have been the largest in Wales with a nave longer than those of Canterbury and Salisbury cathedrals.

RIDING EAST TO WEST

Stock up with snacks before you leave Knighton as the pub-cum-village-shop and post office in Abbey-cwm-hir only does soup or sandwiches by prior arrangement, and there is nothing else until you reach Rhayader.

CROSS ROUTE 5
Fishguard to Carmarthen

Start	Fishguard & Goodwick Railway Station (SM 945 382)
Finish	Carmarthen Railway Station (SN 413 197)
Distance	45 miles (72km)
Ascent	1300m
Time	7–8 hr
OS maps	OS Landranger 157, 145 and 159
Refreshments	The only places for food are the cafés, pubs and shops in Crymych, so top up with supplies before leaving Fishguard
Accommodation	Plenty of B&Bs and hotels in Fishguard and Carmarthen, but only a few B&Bs along the route

This route, which follows NCN 47 for most of the way, is relentlessly undulating, heading first along the Preseli Hills and then through rolling countryside riddled with streams that result in frequent climbs out of the numerous cwms (valleys). However, it also contains glorious countryside and can be linked with the second half of Stage 2 as well as the whole of Stage 3 to make a delightful short tour that starts and finishes in Carmarthen.

Ride along the shared-use path past Ocean Lab Tourist Information Centre and café, climb up the hillside above the A40 and then turn left following signs for NCN 47 and 82 into **Fishguard** (2/43 miles). Ride through the town and out along the B4313, passing through Llanychaer (4/41 miles), with Afon Gwaun below in the valley.

Bear right on a sharp bend where NCN 82 drops down into the Gwaun Valley and continue towards Maenclochog, climbing around **Mynydd Cilciffeth**, which is the westernmost of the Preseli Hills. Although this point is only 270m above sea level, the views over the flatter landscape to the south are quite spectacular as is the descent into **Puncheston** (9/36 miles).

The name of **The Drovers Arms at Puncheston** shows the village was once an important centre for drovers bringing cattle, sheep, pigs and even geese from West Wales through to markets in more populated areas to the south and east. This was a tradition that stretched back to at least the 14th century, when Henry V (1387–1422) ordered large numbers of cattle to be driven from Wales to the Channel Ports to supply his troops in France; the practice only died out with the arrival of the railways in the middle of the 19th century. The inn would have provided drink and food for both the animals and the drovers. However, like most pubs in rural Wales, the inn does not open at lunchtimes during the week, so most likely you will get neither.

Map continues on page 202

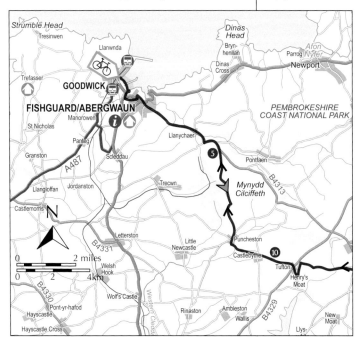

Map continues
on page 205

Less than 1km off
route along the
B4313 in Rosebush
is Tafarn Sinc, a
pub constructed
from corrugated
iron, which opens
at noon every day
except Mondays.

Ride through **Castlebythe** (10/35 miles), which gets its name from the Norman motte and bailey castle alongside the route, and continue to Tufton (11/34 miles). Follow signs for NCN 47 across the B4329 and ride into Henry's Moat, a village that gets its name from an ancient moated tumulus just off route on the right behind the parish church. Turn left at the unmarked junction on the edge of the village and ride uphill back towards the B4329. Turn right just before the junction with the main road and ride through Trebengych (14/31 miles) to meet the **B4313**. Turn left towards Fishguard and then right after 500 metres, heading towards Crymych. ◄

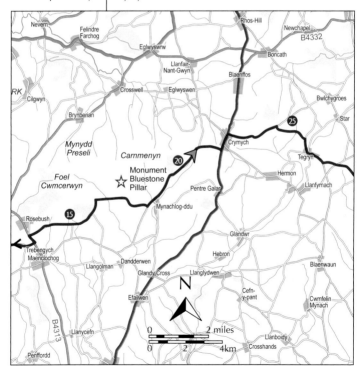

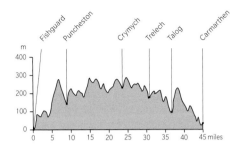

Foel Cwmcerwyn (536m), the highest summit in the Preseli Hills, is just north of the route. After climbing around its lower slopes, the road swings northwards to cross the low-lying scrubland along the banks of Afon Wern. There are numerous standing stones, stone circles and cromlechs scattered across the moorland on either side of the road as well as the **Bluestone Pillar**, which commemorates the fact that some of the bluestones from the inner horseshoe at Stonehenge were quarried at Carn Menyn, which is the crag on the skyline behind it.

Bluestone Pillar with Carn Menyn, where stones for the inner circle of Stonehenge originated, on the skyline

No one is entirely sure how the builders of Stonehenge moved the 3- to 5-ton volcanic bluestone blocks, which form the inner ring of the circle, from **Carn Menyn** and other locations in the Preseli Hills 160 miles (257 km) to Wiltshire. Although geophysical analysis has confirmed that the bluestones came from the area, there are various theories about how they were physically moved.

Some experts believe that the builders used wooden rollers formed from tree trunks laid side by side on a constructed hard surface, while others suggest they used huge wooden sleds on top of greased wooden rails. However, although evidence confirms that the stones were quarried by man, there is another theory that the stones are glacial erratics that were broken off the local crags around half a million years ago by the Irish Sea Glacier and subsequently carried by the ice eastwards towards Salisbury Plain.

Turn left at the next junction and ride through Mynachlog-ddu (20/25 miles) to **Crymych** (23/22 miles). Turn left along the A478, ride down through the village and either grab a snack or stock up on supplies for the remainder of the ride to Carmarthen. When you are ready to go, continue along the A478 and then turn right on the edge of the village, heading towards Tegryn. Climb around the southern flank of Frenni Fawr to an altitude of 290m above sea level, which is the highest point on the route, turn right and right again a mile further on and ride through **Tegryn** (27/18 miles).

Turn left on the outskirts of the village, still following signs for NCN 47. Go straight across the first crossroads and then turn right at the next junction, heading towards Dinas. Ride through **Dinas** (31/14 miles), which is a pleasant little village at the bottom of one of the all too frequent cwms. ◄ Once you have climbed out of this cwm, turn left towards Trelech and then right at the junction in the centre of the village, heading towards Meidrim. After 200 metres of climbing, turn left into a

Marginal deposits of lead were successfully mined in Dinas in the middle of the 19th century when the prices were buoyant due to high demand and the Crimean War limited imports.

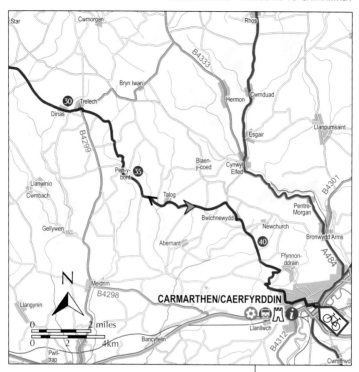

narrow lane and follow waymarker signs across the first crossroads steeply down and around another small cwm 2 miles further on to **Pen-y-bont** (35/10 miles).

Turn left and enjoy 2 miles of fast descent to **Talog** (37/8 miles), then grit your teeth for 1½ miles of climbing up through the trees to a ridge that gives superb views northwards back to the Preseli Hills. Turn right at the next T-junction, leaving NCN 47, which continues beyond Carmarthen only to loop back into the town from the east. Ride through Bwlchnewydd (40/5 miles) and then 1 mile after passing the Plough and Harrow Inn turn right into Nantybwlya Road. At its end, turn left, ride down Heol Pentrehydd and then turn right along Jacob's Well

A happy cyclist ambles along the road south of the Preseli Hills

Road. Turn left along Monument Road, ride past the monument and then turn right by the Welsh Government office to join NCN 4. The Duke of Wellington called Sir Thomas Picton (1758–1815), whose death at the battle of Waterloo is commemorated by the prominent monument in Monument Road, 'a rough foul-mouthed devil as ever lived'. Follow NCN 4 around the perimeter of Carmarthen Park and across Afon Tywi to Carmarthen Railway Station where the route ends.

RIDING EAST TO WEST

Stock up with snacks before you leave Carmarthen, as there is nowhere for a break until you reach Crymych after 22 miles of continually undulating riding.

CROSS ROUTE 6
Carmarthen to Abergavenny

Start	Carmarthen Railway Station (SN 413 197)
Finish	Abergavenny Railway Station (SO 305 136)
Distance	70 miles (112km)
Ascent	1400m
Time	10–11 hr
OS maps	OS Landranger 159, 160 and 161
Refreshments	Between Ffairfach and Brecon the only shops, pubs or cafés are in Sennybridge or just off route in Trecastle
Accommodation	Hostels at Llanddeusant, Brecon and Llangattock, and plenty of other choices in the major towns along the route

This quiet route goes around the north of the Brecon Beacons. First it follows NCN 47 out of Carmarthen and then the 'Cycle across the Beacons' trail all the way to Abergavenny. The 'Cycle across the Beacons' trail currently starts at Llandeilo but will soon be extended back into Carmarthen once work is completed on a traffic-free path along the disused track of a branch line that ran between Carmarthen and Llandeilo. The 'Cycle across the Beacons' trail is well waymarked with orange stickers.

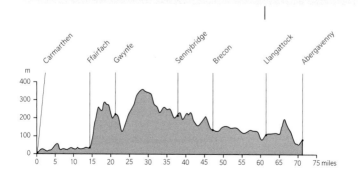

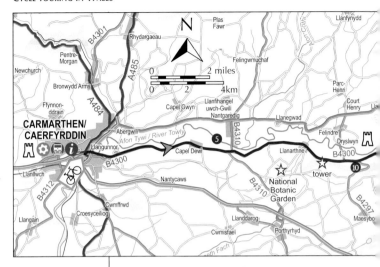

The National Botanic Garden of Wales, 2 miles south of Llanarthne, has wonderful themed gardens, the world's largest single-span glasshouse and a tropical butterfly house.

Once out of the station turn immediately right down the ramp following signs for NCN 47 and pass under the A484 and along Hen Heol Llangynnwr past the bike shop. Leave the road on the corner and follow a shared-use path under the A40 flyover. Turn left along the B4300 and follow it through **Llanarthne** (8/62 miles), where NCN 47 turns south. ◀ The River Towy meanders through the pastureland down in the valley to your left and the Brecon Beacons are straight ahead.

Situated majestically on a hilltop on the opposite side of the valley, **Dryslwyn Castle** was built in the first quarter of the 13th century by one of the Welsh princes of the kingdom of Deheubarth. Because it was built by a Welsh chieftain (rather than an English king) and is still remarkably intact, it is an important Grade I listed building.

Further up the valley, 1½ miles off route, are **Aberglasney Gardens**, which were planted in the early years of the 20th century by Colonel Charles Mayhew. A succession of different owners

Map continues on page 210

There are plenty of antiquities to look at along the way too. Paxton's Tower, above Llanarthne, is a neo-Gothic folly erected during the first decade of the 19th century by the wealthy merchant Sir William Paxton (1745–1824) to honour Lord Nelson. Paxton built and lived at the nearby Middleton Hall and invested in many local schemes, including the development of Tenby as a resort. Middleton Hall was destroyed by fire in 1931, but his estate became the site of the National Botanic Garden of Wales.

repeatedly remodelled the original medieval house, but by the middle of the 20th century the house was derelict and the gardens overgrown. Intervention by the Welsh Office led to the establishment of the Aberglasney Restoration Trust, which has restored both the house and gardens to their former splendour, aided by a generous endowment from the late American financier and fanatical horticulturalist Francis Higginson Cabot (1925–2011).

Paxton's Tower standing high above the Towy Valley

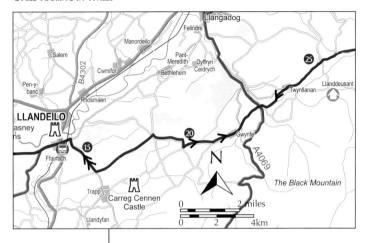

Map continues
on page 212

Just before Llandeilo you may catch sight of a second hilltop castle.

This is **Dinefwr Castle**, which legend has it was originally built by Rhodri the Great (c. 820–878), who ruled over much of modern Wales. However, little remains from this period and what remains of the castle is thought to have been built by Rhys ap Gruffydd (1132–1197), who today is commonly referred to as simply Lord Rhys. Rhys ruled over most of Wales during the second half of the 12th century and famously made peace with King Henry II (1171–1188) until the latter's death after which Rhys resumed hostilities against his successor Richard I. Again, because Dinefwr represents the significant remains of a castle built by a Welsh prince, it carries a Grade I listing. There is another one a few miles further along the route.

Llandeilo, the last place to buy supplies before Brecon, is a pretty market town with brightly painted houses along the main street and an eclectic mix of shops and cafés.

Continue along the B4300 to its end. Turn left along the A476 and then after 1km cross the A483 and ride into **Ffairfach** (14/56 miles), which is just across the river from Llandeilo. ◄ Go under the railway and across the river

210

Carreg Cennen Castle, which is spectacularly set on a limestone crag above the River Cennen, is often said to be the most beautiful castle in Wales

and then turn right towards **Trap** – the trap being having to climb the hillside for 2 miles at an average gradient of 7%! Turn left towards Bethlehem at the crossroads at the top and enjoy riding along the ridge with magnificent views northwards across the Towy Valley to the Cambrian Mountains and southwards across the Cennen Valley to Black Mountain. ▶ Turn right at the next crossroads, heading towards Gwynfe. After 250 metres turn left, still heading for Gwynfe and ride through **Gwynfe** (21/49 miles). As the road bends around to the left, go straight on taking the narrow road to the left of the farmyard and descend to meet the A4069. Cross at the bridge into the lane opposite, then 200 metres further on, turn left into a narrow lane with a sign warning that it is unsuitable for heavy goods vehicles. You will soon find out why when you come to a steep switchback where you may need to dismount and walk.

Climb gently up to **Twynllanan** (24/46 miles) and then turn right towards Trecastle. Continue climbing up past The Red Kite Inn at Talsarn (26/44 miles). ▶ The next 2 miles of road across the open moor are almost perfectly straight, betraying its Roman origins and there was once

Carreg Cennen Castle, which is spectacularly set on a limestone crag above the River Cennen, is also thought to have been built by Lord Rhys.

At the red kite feeding station just 300 metres off route north of Talsarn towards Myddfai, you can see 50+ red kite being fed at 3.00pm BST or 2.00pm GMT.

211

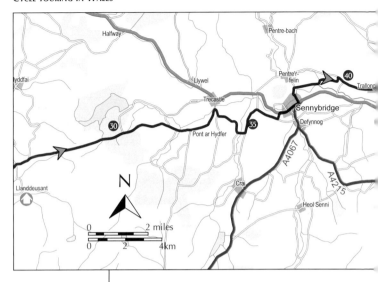

Map continues
on page 215

a Roman camp just off it to the south. At about 1100ft
(340m) above sea level, this is now the highest point
of the route, giving wonderful views northwards to the
Cambrian Mountains.

Descend through **Pont ar Hydfer** (32/38 miles) and
then a mile further on, just before the bridge over the River
Usk near Trecastle, turn right towards Defynnog. Follow
the road around into Cwm Crai and turn left towards
Sennybridge. After 2 miles turn left along the A4067 and
left again into Heol Defynnog just 200 metres later. Ride
through **Sennybridge** (37/33 miles), turning right along
High Street and then 250 metres later turn left towards
Pentre'r-felin. Six hundred metres after crossing the River
Usk, turn right and follow this narrow lane for 2 miles
with the River Usk down to your right. Turn right towards
Trallong at the next junction and ride through Trallong
(42/28 miles), **Aberbran** (43/27 miles) and Aberyscir (44/26
miles) to Cradoc (45/25 miles). Turn right in the centre of
the village and ride down to **Brecon** (47/23 miles), with
the Brecon Beacons strung out along the southern horizon.

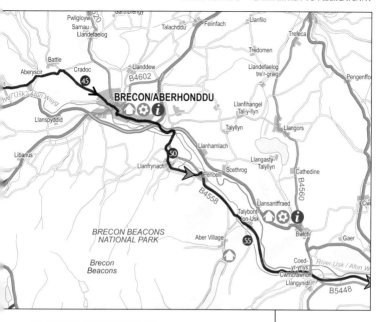

BRECON

Brecon is a thriving little town that probably became established due to it being one of the few places where the river could be forded. Its Welsh name – Aberhonddu – is derived from the River Honddu, which meets the River Usk near the town centre. The Normans built a castle on the hill and defensive walls around the town, but they were largely destroyed during the English Civil War. Once Brecknockshire was absorbed into Powys in 1974, Brecon lost its status as a county town, but it remains a thriving community with an important cattle market and plenty to entertain the large influx of tourists who flock into the area. Their numbers are boosted in early August when the town hosts the internationally acclaimed Brecon Jazz Festival. See www.breconjazz.org for details.

Brecon lies at the north of the Brecon Beacons National Park. The park was established in 1957 and covers 519 square miles. It stretches from Llandeilo in the west to Hay-on-Wye in the north-east and Pontypool in the south-east.

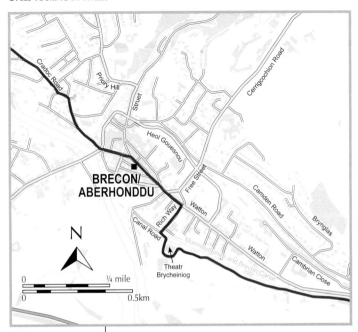

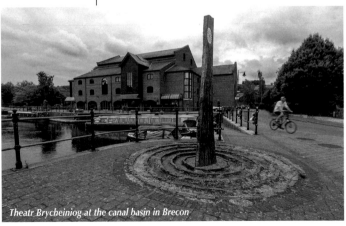

Theatr Brycheiniog at the canal basin in Brecon

Ride through the town centre, past the Breckon Museum and Art Gallery and then turn right along Rich Way, following signs for NCN 8. Turn left at the mini roundabout at its end and ride around Theatr Brycheiniog to pick up the towpath alongside the Monmouthshire and Brecon Canal. After two miles leave the canal and turn right along the B4558, following waymarker signs for NCN 8. Cross the River Usk and then turn right towards Llanfrynach. Ride through **Llanfrynach** (50/20 miles) and Pencelli (52/18 miles), where the route rejoins the B4558. NCN 8 turns right at the junction by the war memorial in the hamlet of Cross Oak and heads down the Taff Valley to Cardiff, but our route continues along the B4558 following waymarker signs for 'Cycle across the Beacons'.

Ride through Talybont-on-Usk (54/16 miles) and **Llangynidr** (57/13 miles) with the Black Mountains to your left and the Brecon Beacons to your right trapping the canal and the River Usk in a narrowing valley. After 4 miles turn right towards Dardy and then immediately right on the bend and left at the next junction and ride up to Dardy (61/9 miles) to join the towpath along the

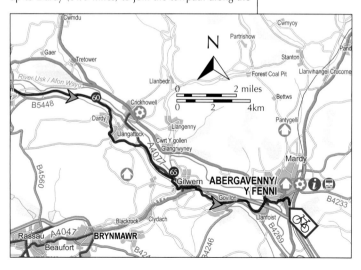

During the 19th century limestone quarried from the imposing Llangattock Escarpment was carried on the canal to steelworks further down the Usk Valley.

Monmouthshire and Brecon Canal. Follow the towpath along the hillside for 6 miles, passing **Llangattock** (62/8 miles) and its larger neighbour Crickhowell, which is a mile off route on the opposite bank of the River Usk. ◄

Ride through **Gilwern** (65/5 miles), where the route crosses over the famous A465 Head of the Valleys road to Govilon (67/3 miles) where the route leaves the towpath. Turn right following waymarker signs for 'Cycle across the Beacons', cycle up Station Road for 100 metres and turn left along a shared-use path that runs downhill along the course of the long disused tramway, which used to carry limestone, coal and iron between Blaenavon and wharves in Llanfoist (69/1 miles).

Turn left along the B4264 and then 200 metres further on turn left along The Cutting, following waymarker signs for 'Cycle across the Beacons'. Ride under the Head of the Valleys, around the busy roundabout at the north of the village and across the River Usk. Cross the carriageway and follow a shared-use path through Castle Meadows into Abergavenny. When you reach the ruins of Abergavenny Castle, turn right and follow waymarker signs for 'Cycle across the Beacons' around into Mill Street. Cross Monmouth Road and then turn right into Holywell Road, which leads around to **Abergavenny Railway Station** where the route ends.

RIDING EAST TO WEST

Unless you want to dismount and walk through Brecon town centre, you will need to bear left behind Brecon Museum and Art Gallery and follow the one-way system along Glamorgan Street and Wheat Street before turning left into Ship Street and riding out of the town.

APPENDIX A

Cycle shops

The following is a list of cycle shops on or near the routes in this guidebook.

Abergavenny

Gateway Cycles
5 Brecon Road
Abergavenny NP7 5UH
tel 01873 858 519
www.gatewaycycles.co.uk

Aberystwyth

Halfords
3, Parc y Llyn Retail Park
Llanbadarn Fawr
Aberystwyth SY23 3TL
tel 01970 627187
www.halfords.com

Summit Cycles
65 North Parade
Aberystwyth SY23 2JN
tel 01970 626061
www.summitcycles.co.uk

Bala

R.H. Roberts Cycles
7/9 High Street
Bala LL23 7AG
tel 01678 520252
www.rhrcycles.magix.net/public

Bangor

Evolution Bikes
Cyttir Lane
Bangor LL57 4DA
tel 01248 355 770
www.evolution-bikes.co.uk

Barry

Halfords
Waterfront Retail Park
The Waterfront
Barry CF63 4BA
tel 01446 731000
www.halfords.com

Betws-y-Coed

Beics Betws
Holyhead Road
Betws-y-Coed
LL24 0AB
tel 01690 710766
www.bikewales.co.uk

Brecon

Bi Ped Cycles
10 Ship Street
Brecon LD3 9AF
tel 01874 622 296
www.bipedcycles.co.uk

Caernarfon

Beics Menai Bikes
1 Cei Llechi
Caernarfon LL55 2PB
tel 01286 676 804

Cardigan

New Image Bicycles
29–30 Pendre
Cardigan SA43 1LA
tel 01239 621275
www.bikebikebike.co.uk

Cardiff

Bike Shed Wales
2B Merthyr Road
Tongwynlais
Cardiff CF15 7LF
tel 0292 081 1870
www.bikeshedwales.com

Cyclopaedia Ltd
116 Crwys Road
Cardiff CF24 4NR
tel 0292 037 7772
www.cyclopaedia.co.uk

Damian Harris Cycles
55 Merthyr Road
Cardiff CF14 1DD
tel 0292 0529 955
www.damianharriscycles.co.uk

Evans Cycles
Dumfries Place
Cardiff CF10 3FN
tel 0292 097 2700
www.evanscycles.com/store/cardiff

Outdoor Cycles
82 Pwllmelin Road
Cardiff CF5 2NH
tel 0292 056 4367
www.outdoorcycles.co.uk/

plan2ride Bike Café
Rear of, 51 Merthyr Road
Tongwynlais
Cardiff CF15 7LG
tel 0292 081 0868
www.plan2ride.co.uk

Sunset Cycles
119–121 Woodville Road
Cardiff CF24 4DZ
tel 0292 039 0883
www.sunsetmtb.co.uk

Carmarthen

Beiciau Hobbs Bikes
Old Station Road
Carmarthen SA31 2BD
tel 01267 236785

Cefn-mawr

Derek's Cycles
Well Street
Cefn-mawr LL14 3AE
tel 01978 821841

Coed-y-Brenin

Beics Brenin
Coed Y Brenin Visitor Centre
Dolgellau LL40 2HZ
tel 01341 440728
www.beicsbrenin.co.uk

Colwyn Bay

East End Cycles
93 Abergele Road
Colwyn Bay L29 7SA
tel 01492 533834

Crickhowell

Bike Anatomy
Riverside Business Center
New Road
Crickhowell NP8 1AY
tel 01873 811199
www.bikeanatomy.com

Dolgellau

Dolgellau Cycles
The Old Furnace
Smithfield Street
Dolgellau LL40 1DF
tel 01341 423332
www.dolgellaucycles.co.uk

Dunvant

The Bike Bloke (mobile service)
Yr Elain, Dunvant
Swansea
tel 07876 573879
www.thebikebloke.com

Haverfordwest

Mikes Bikes
17 Prendergast
Haverfordwest SA61 2PE
tel 01437 760068
www.mikes-bikes.co.uk

Halfords
1 Meadow Walk
Haverfordwest SA61 2EX
tel 01437 767313
www.halfords.com

Hay-on-Wye

Drover Cycles
Forest Road
Hay-on-Wye HR3 5EH
tel 01497 822 419 or 07501 495 868
www.drovercycles.co.uk

Holywell

Life on Wheels
Hillcrest Garage
Halkyn Road
Holywell CH8 7SJ
tel 01352 715716
www.lifeonwheels.co.uk

Kington

Behind Bars
15 Tan House Meadows
Kington HR5 3TD
tel 01544 230283
www.behind-bars.biz

Llanbedr

Snowdonia Cycles
Llanbedr LL45 2HN
tel 01341 241 916
www.snowdoniacycles.co.uk

Llandudno Junction

West End Cycles
Conwy Road
Llandudno Junction LL31 9BA
tel 01492 593811
www.westendcycles.com

Llanelli

Halfords
10b, Parc Pemberton Retail Park (A484)
Llanelli SA14 9UZ
tel 01554 785980
www.halfords.com

Llangollen

Llan Velo
1–3 Berwyn Street
Llangollen LL20 8NF
tel 01978 806226
www.llanvelo.co.uk

Llangynidr

Cycle Basket
Waterloo House
Cwm Crawnon Road, Llangynidr
Crickhowell NP8 1LS
tel 01874 730368
www.cyclebasket.com

Newport

South Wales Bikes
45 Caerleon Road
Newport NP19 7BW
tel 01633 243384
www.southwalesbikes.co.uk

Oswestry

BikeWorks
95 Beatrice Street
Oswestry SY11 1HL
tel 01691 654407
www.bikeworksoswestry.co.uk

Halfords
2 Penda Retail Park
Salop Road
Oswestry SY11 2RL
tel 01691 677920
www.halfords.com

Pembroke Dock

Bierspool Cycles
58 London Road
Pembroke Dock SA72 6DT
tel 01646 681039
www.bierspoolcycles.co.uk

Penarth

The Bike Shop Wales
86 Glebe Street
Penarth CF64 1EF
tel 02920 704 524
www.thebikeshopwales.co.uk

Tredz Bikes
2 Penarth Road Retail Park
Penarth
Llandough
Cardiff CF11 8EF
tel 0292 070 2229
www.tredz.co.uk

Porthmadog

K K Cycles
141 High Street
Porthmadog LL49 9HD
tel 01766 512 310

Port Talbot

Re: Cycles Workshop
Kenfig Industrial Estate
Port Talbot SA13 2PE
tel 07971 838842
www.recycles.wales

Lodge Cycles
The Old Telephone Exchange
Depot Road, Cwmavon
Port Talbot SA12 9DF
tel 01639 886139
www.lodgecycles.co.uk

Welsh Coast Cycles
34 Forge Road
Port Talbot SA13 1NU
tel 01639 894169
www.welshcoastcycles.co.uk

Presteigne

Chris's Cycles
Horseyard House (B4357)
Presteigne LD8 2SA
tel 07970 152170
www.chrisscycles.co.uk

Dream Pedaller
High Street
Presteigne LD8 2BA
tel 07531 672 113
www.dreampedallers.co.uk

Rhayader

Elan Cyclery
West Street
Rhayader LD6 5AB
tel 01597 811 343
www.clivepowell-mtb.co.uk

Rhyl

The Bike Hub
Foryd Harbour
Rhyl L18 5AX
tel 01745 339758
www.bikehubrhyl.uk

Shotton

Graham Weigh Cycles
3/5 Chester Road East
Shotton CH5 1QA
tel 01244 831110
www.grahamweighcycles.co.uk

Shotton Cycles
24 Chester Road East
Shotton CH5 1QA
tel 01244 836583
www.shottoncycles.co.uk

Swansea

Pilot House Cycles
Pilot House Wharf
Swansea SA1 1UN
tel 01792 463199
www.pilothousecycles.co.uk

The Bike Hub
78 St Helen's Road
Swansea
tel 01792 466944
www.thebikehub.co.uk

Talybont-on-Usk

Bikes & Hikes
Talybont-on-Usk
Brecon LD3 7YJ
tel 07909 968 135
www.bikesandhikes.co.uk

Welshpool

Brooks Cycles
Severn Street
Welshpool SY21 7AB
tel 01938 553582
www.brookscycles.co.uk

Wrexham

Alf Jones Cycles
82 Chester Road
Gresford
Wrexham LL12 8NT
tel 01978 854300
www.alfjonescycles.co.uk

Bike Shop
Stansty Road
Wrexham LL11 2DD
tel 01978 354429
www.bikeshopwrexham.co.uk

Setchfield Cycles
12 Two Mile Industrial Estate
Quarry Road
Pentre Broughton
Wrexham LL11 6AB
tel 01978 447200
www.setchfieldcycles.co.uk

APPENDIX B
Accommodation

Selected hotels and B&Bs
This selection lists cycle-friendly hotels and B&Bs located at the beginning and end of each Stage and Cross route.

Aberaeron
Carno House B&B
North Parade
Aberaeron
Ceredigion SA46 OJP
tel 01545 571862
www.carnohouse.com

Abergavenny
Park Guest House
36 Hereford Road
Abergavenny NP7 5RA
tel 01873 853715
www.parkguesthouse.co.uk

Aberystwyth
Queensbridge Hotel
Victoria Terrace
Aberystwyth SY23 2DH
tel 01970 612343
www.queensbridgehotel.com

Bangor
Plas Trevor B&B
Victoria Drive
Bangor LL57 2EN
tel 01248 371377
www.plastrevor.co.uk

Cardiff
Future Inn
Hemingway Road
Cardiff CF10 4AU
tel 02920 487111
www.futureinns.co.uk

Carmarthen
Old Priory Guest House
20 Priory Street
Carmarthen SA31 1NE
tel 01267 237471
www.oldprioryguesthouse.com

Chepstow
The Woodfield Arms
16 Bridge Street, Chepstow
Monmouthshire NP16 5EZ
tel 01291 620349
www.thewoodfieldarms.com

Chirk
The Hand Hotel
Church Street
Chirk LL14 5EY
tel 01691 773472
www.thehandhotelchirk.co.uk

Conwy
Glan Heulog B&B
Llanrwst Road
Glan Heulog
Conwy LL32 8LT
tel 01492 593845
www.conwy-bedandbreakfast.co.uk

Fishguard
Fern Villa B&B
Church Road, Goodwick
Fishguard SA64 0EH
www.fernvillafishguard.co.uk

Hay-on-Wye
The Start B&B
Hay-on-Wye HR3 5RS
tel 01497 821391
www.the-start.net

Machynlleth
Dyfiview B&B
21 Ffordd Mynydd Griffiths
Machynlleth SY20 8DD
tel 01654 702023/07952 370569
www.dyfiview.co.uk

Montgomery
Dragon Hotel
Market Square
Montgomery SY15 6PA
tel 01686 668359
www.dragonhotel.com

Mumbles
Leonardo's Guest House
380 Oystermouth Road
Swansea SA1 3UL
tel 01792 470163
www.leonardosguesthouse.co.uk

Porthmadog
Gwynfa B&B
Penamser Road
Porthmadog LL49 9NY
tel 01766 512959/07581 314484
www.gwynfabandb.co.uk

Tenby
Pen Mar Guest House
New Hedges
Tenby SA70 8TL
tel 01834 842435
www.penmar-tenby.co.uk

Welshpool
Tynllwyn Farm
Welshpool SY21 9BW
tel 01938 553175
www.tynllwynfarm.co.uk

Wrexham
Woodhey Guest House
9 Sontley Road
Wrexham LL13 7EN
tel 01978 262555
www.woodhey-guesthouse.com

Hostels and bunkhouses

Abergavenny
The Great Western
24 Station Road
Abergavenny NP7 5HS
tel 01873 859125
www.greatwesternabergavenny.com

Abersoch (Llyn Peninsula)
Abersoch Sgubor Unnos
Fferm Tanrallt Farm
Llangian, Abersoch
Gwynedd LL53 7LN
tel 01758 713527
www.abersoch-tanrallt.co.uk

Aberystwyth
Plas Dolau Country House Hostel
Lovesgrove
Aberystwyth SY23 3HP
tel 01970 617834
www.plasdolau.co.uk
(3 miles off route)

Bala
Bala Backpackers
2 Tegid Street
Bala LL23 7EL
tel 01678 521700
www.bala-backpackers.co.uk

Bala Bunkhouse
Tomen Y Castell
Llanfor
Bala LL23 7HD
tel 01678 520738
www.balabunkhouse.co.uk

Barmouth
Bunkorama
Off Panorama Road
Barmouth
Gwynedd LL42 1DX
tel 01341 281134/07738 467196
www.bunkorama.co.uk
Up a steep hill above the town

Bethesda
Caban Cysgu Gerlan Bunkhouse
Ffordd Gerlan
Gerlan, Bethesda
Bangor LL57 3ST
tel 01248 605573/07464 676753
www.cabancysgu-gerlan.co.uk

Betws-y-Coed

Vagabond Bunkhouse
Craiglan
Betws-y-Coed
Conwy LL24 0AW
tel 01690 710850 or 07816 076546
www.thevagabond.co.uk

YHA Betws-y-Coed
Swallow Falls
Betws-y-Coed LL24 0DW
tel 01690 710796
www.yha.org.uk

Borth
YHA Borth
Morlais
Borth
Ceredigion SY24 5JS
tel 01970 871498
www.yha.org.uk

Broad Haven
YHA Broad Haven
Broad Haven SA62 3JH
tel 0345 371 9008
www.yha.org.uk

Bwlch
The Star Bunkhouse
Brecon Road (A40)
Bwlch
Brecon LD3 7RQ
tel 01874 730080/07341 906937
www.starbunkhouse.com

Caernarfon
Totters
Plas Porth Yr Aur
2 High Street
Caernarfon
Gwynedd LL55 1RN
tel 01286 672963/07979 830470
www.totters.co.uk

Capel Curig
Plas Curig
Capel Curig LL24 0EL
tel 01690 720225
www.therockshostel.com

Cardiff
River House Hostel
59 Fitzhamon Embankment
Riverside
Cardiff CF11 6AN
tel 02920 399810
www.riverhousebackpackers.com

Safehouse Hostel
3 Westgate Street
Cardiff CF10 1DD
tel 02920 372833
www.the-safehouse-hostel.cardiff-
hotels.co.uk

YHA Cardiff Central
East Tyndall Street
Cardiff CF10 4BB
tel 03453 719311
www.yha.org.uk

Cardigan
Piggery Poke Hostel
Ffrwdwenith Isaf
Felinwynt
Cardigan SA43 1RW
tel 01239 811777
www.piggerypoke.co.uk

Cefn-brith
Tyddyn Bychan
Cefn Brith
Conwy LL21 9TS
tel 01490 420680 or 07523 995741
www.bunkhousenorthwales.co.uk

Chepstow
Green Man Backpackers
13 Beaufort Square
Chepstow NP16 5EP
tel 01291 626773
www.greenmanbackpackers.co.uk

Conwy
YHA Conwy
Sychnant Pass Road
Conwy LL32 8AJ
tel 0345 371 9732
www.yha.org.uk

Dolgellau
Hyb Bunkhouse
2–3 Heol y Bont (Bridge Street
Dolgellau
Gwynedd LL40 1AU
tel 01341 421755

Dylife
Y Star Inn Bunkhouse
Dylife
Llanbrynmair
Powys SY19 7BW
tel 01650 521345
www.starinndylife.co.uk

Fishguard
Hamilton Backpackers
23 Hamilton Street
Fishguard SA65 9HL
tel 07505 562939
www.hamiltonbackpackers.co.uk

James John Hamilton House
19a Hamilton Street
Fishguard SA65 9HL
tel 01348 874288
www.jamesjohnhamilton.co.uk

Garndolbenmaen
Cwm Pennant Hostel
Golan
Garndolbenmaen
Gwynedd LL51 9AQ
tel 01766 530888/01706 877320

Glasbury
Woodlands Bunkhouse
Glasbury on Wye HR3 5LP
tel 01497 847272
www.independenthostels.co.uk/
members/woodlandsbunkhouse/

Holyhead (Anglesey)
Anglesey Outdoor Centre
Porthdafarch Road
Holyhead LL65 2LP
tel 01407 769351
www.angleseyoutdoors.com

Kington
YHA Kington
Kington
Herefordshire HR5 3BX
tel 0345 371 9053
www.yha.org.uk

Llanddeusant
YHA Llanddeusant
Llanddeusant
Carmarthenshire SA19 9UL
tel 0345 371 9750
www.yha.org.uk
(Take food as the nearest shop or pub is
8 miles away)

Llandudno
Llandudno Hostel
14 Charlton Street
Llandudno LL30 2AA
tel 01492 877430
www.llandudnohostel.co.uk

Llangattock
YHA Llangattock Mountain Bunkhouse
Llangattock
Crickhowell NP8 1LG
tel 0800 0191 700
www.yha.org.uk

Llanidloes
Plasnewydd Bunkhouse
Gorn Road, Llanidloes
Powys SY18 6LA
tel 01686 412431/07975 913049
www.plasnewyddbunkhouse.co.uk

Llanellen
Middle Ninfa Bunkhouse
Llanellen
Abergavenny NP7 9LE
tel 01873 854662
www.middleninfa.co.uk
Two miles up a steep lane above
Llanfoist

Llangollen
Llangollen Hostel
Berwyn Street
Llangollen LL20 8NB
tel 01978 861773
www.llangollenhostel.co.uk

Llanrhystud
Morfa Farm Bunkhouse
LLanrhystud
Ceredigion SY23 5BU
tel 01974 202253
www.morfafarm.co.uk

Llansteffan
Pantyrathro International Hostel
Llansteffan
Carmarthen SA33 5AJ
tel 01267 241014
www.backpackershostelwales.com

Machynlleth
Toad Hall
Doll Street
Machynlleth
Powys SY20 8BH
tel 01654 700597/07866 362507

Manorbier
YHA Manorbier
Manorbier SA70 7TT
tel 0345 371 9031
www.yha.org.uk

Newport
YHA Newport
Lower St Mary Street
Newport
Pembrokeshire SA42 0TS
tel 0345 371 9543
www.yha.org.uk

Ogwen Valley
YHA Idwal
Nant Ffrancon
Bethesda
Bangor LL57 3LZ
tel 0345 371 9744
www.yha.org.uk

Oxwich (Gower)
Eastern Slade Barn
Oxwich
Swansea SA3 1NA
tel 07970 969814
www.easternsladebarngower.co.uk

Pantygelli
Smithy's Bunkhouse
Lower House Farm
Pantygelli
Abergavenny NP7 7HR
tel 01873 853432
www.smithysbunkhouse.co.uk

Poppit Sands
YHA Poppit Sands
Poppit
Cardigan SA43 3LP
tel 0345 371 9037
www.yha.org.uk

Port Eynon (Gower)
YHA Port Eynon
Port Eynon
Swansea SA3 1NN
tel 0345 371 9135
www.yha.org.uk

Port Talbot
L & A Outdoor Centre
Goytre
West Glamorgan SA13 2YP
tel 01639 885509
www.landaoutdoorcentre.co.uk

Pwllheli (Llyn Peninsula)
Aberdaron Farm Bunkhouse
Y Gweithdy
Anelog, Aberdaron
Pwllheli LL53 8BT
tel 0779 414 7195
www.aberdaronfarmholidays.co.uk

Rhayader
Beili Neuadd Bunkhouse
Beili Neuadd
Rhayader
Powys LD6 5NS
tel 01597 810211
www.beilineuadd.co.uk

Rhoscolyn (Anglesey)
Outdoor Alternative
Cerrig-yr-Adar
Rhoscolyn
Holyhead LL65 2NQ
tel 01407 860469
www.outdooralternative.co.uk

Rhossili (Gower)
Rhossili Bunkhouse
Rhossili
Swansea SA3 1PL
tel 01792 391509
www.rhossilibunkhouse.com

YHA Rhossili
Rhossili
Swansea SA3 1PJ
tel 03452 603107
www.yha.org.uk

St David's
YHA St David's
Llaethdy
Whitesands
St David's SA62 6PR
tel 0345 371 9141
www.yha.org.uk

St Harmon
Mid Wales Bunkhouse
(5 miles off route)
Woodhouse Farm
St Harmon
Rhayader LD6 5LY
tel 01597 870081
www.bunkhousemidwales.co.uk

Staylittle
Hafren Forest Bunkhouse
Staylittle
Powys SY19 7DB
tel 07871 740514

Talybont-on-Usk
The White Hart Inn & Bunkhouse
Talybont-On-Usk
Brecon LD3 7JD
tel 01874 676227
www.whitehartinntalybont.co.uk

YHA Brecon Beacons
Danywenallt
Talybont-on-Usk
Brecon
Powys LD3 7YS
tel 0345 371 9548
www.yha.org.uk

Trefin
Caerhafod Lodge
Caerhafod
Nr Trefin SA62 5BD
tel 01348 837859
www.caerhafod.co.uk

Old School Hostel
Ffordd-yr-Afon
Trefin SA62 5AU
tel 01348 831800
www.oldschoolhostel.com

Trefasser
YHA Pwll Deri
Castell Mawr
Trefasser
Goodwick SA64 0LR
tel 0345 371 9536
www.yha.org.uk

Campsites
The following organizations have websites that list campsites in Wales:

The Camping and Caravanning Club
www.campingandcaravanningclub.co.uk

Cool Camping
www.coolcamping.co.uk

UK Campsite
www.ukcampsite.co.uk

APPENDIX C
Useful contacts

Tourist information centres
For more information on accommodation, travel and other services, contact the nearest Travel Information Centre or visit www.visitwales.com

Aberaeron
Pen Cei
Aberaeron SA46 0BT
tel 01545 570602

Aberdovey (seasonal)
Wharf Gardens
Aberdovey LL35 0EE
tel 01654 767321

Abergavenny
Swan Meadow, Monmouth Road
Abergavenny NP7 5HF
tel 01873 853254

Aberystwyth
Terrace Road
Aberystwyth SY23 2AG
tel 01970 612125

Barmouth (seasonal)
The Old Library
Station Road, Barmouth
tel 01341 280787

Betws-y-Coed
Royal Oak Stables
Betws-y-Coed LL24 0AH
tel 01690 710426

Brecon
Cattle Market
Brecon LD3 9DA
tel 01874 622485

Caernarfon
Oriel Pendeitsh, Castle Ditch
Caernarfon LL55 1ES
tel 01286 672232

Cardiff
The Old Library
9–11 The Hayes
Cardiff CF10 1AH
tel 0870 121 1258

Pier Head
Cardiff Bay CF10 5AL
tel 029 2046 3833

Cardigan
Theatr Mwldan
Cardigan SA43 2JY
tel 01239 613230

Carmarthen
Castle House & Gaol
Carmarthen Castle
tel 01267 231557

Chepstow
Bridge Street
Chepstow NP16 5EY
tel 01291 623772

Conwy
Muriau Buildings
Rose Hill Street
Conwy LL32 8LD
tel: 01492 577566

Dolgellau
Ty Meirion, Eldon Square
Dolgellau LL40 1LU
tel 01341 422888

Fishguard
Town Hall
Fishguard SA65 9HE
tel 01437 764551

Harlech (seasonal)
Llys Y Graig, High Street
Harlech LL46 2YE
tel 01766 780658

Hay-on-Wye
Oxford Road
Hay-on-Wye HR3 5DG
tel 01497 820144

Holyhead
Terminal 1, Stena Line Port
Holyhead LL65 1DQ
tel 01407 762622

Llandudno
Unit 26 Victoria Centre
Mostyn Street
Llandudno LL30 2RP
tel: 01492 577577

Llanfair Pwllgwyngyll
Station Site
Llanfair Pwllgwyngyll LL61 5UJ
tel 01248 713177

Llangollen
Y Capel,
Castle Street
Llangollen LL20 8NY
tel 01978 860828

Llanidloes
The Library, Mount Lane
Llandiloes SY18 6EY
tel 01686 412855

New Quay
Church Street
New Quay SA45 9NZ
tel 01545 560865

Porthmadog
High Street
Porthmadog LL49 9LD
tel 01766 512981

Rhayader
The Leisure Centre
Rhayader LD6 5BU
tel 01982 553307

Rhyl
The Village, West Parade
Rhyl LL18 1HZ
tel 01745 344515

St David's
Oriel y Parc
St David's SA62 6NW
tel 01437 720392

Tenby
Upper Park Road
Tenby SA70 7LT
tel 01437 775603

Welshpool
Vicarage Garden, Church Street
Welshpool SY21 7DD
tel 01938 552043

Wrexham
Lambpit Street
Wrexham LL11 1AR
tel 01978 292015

APPENDIX D
What to take

Below is a checklist of things to take, along with the typical weights of each item.

Riding gear
- Helmet
- Balaclava or neck tube
- Cycling glasses
- S/S base layer
- S/S cycling jersey
- Arm warmers
- Cycling gloves
- Cycling shorts
- Leg warmers
- Socks
- Waterproof Jacket (350g)
- W/P overtrousers (300g)
- Overshoes (150g)

Leisurewear
- Long-sleeved T-shirt x 2 (150g x 2)
- Underwear x 2 (100g x 2)
- Micro-fleece top (420g)
- Travel trousers (450g)
- Socks x 2 (60g x 2)
- Trainers/Crocs (600g)
- Stuff bag x 2 (40g x 2)

Additional leisurewear for cooler months
- Fleece jacket (550g)
- Heavier travel trousers (550g)

Tools and accessories
- Rear light (55g)
- Front light (100g)
- Pump (110g)
- Multi-tool (120g)

- Spoke key (17g)
- Spare inner tube (120g)
- Spare folding tyre or a 'boot' – section of old tyre for reinforcing splits and holes (350g/50g)
- Self-adhesive patches (20g)
- Tyre levers (26g)
- Powerlink (5g)
- Set of cables (50g)
- Latex gloves (3g)
- Spare bolts x 2 (4g)
- Cable ties x 2 (3g)
- Insulating tape or duct tape (30g)

Extras
- Toiletries (250g)
- Travel towel (135g)
- Sun cream (45g)
- Lip salve (15g)
- Wet wipes (50g)
- Compact first aid kit (200g)
- Map or GPS and charger (150g)
- Guidebook (235g)
- Itinerary (10g)
- Pen (10g)
- Compact camera (265g)
- Phone and charger (270g)
- Wallet/cards (100g)

APPENDIX E

Welsh words and pronunciation

Common Welsh words found in place names

Welsh	English
Welsh	English
aber	river mouth or estuary
afon	river
bach	small, little
bangor	monastery
bedd	grave
betws	chapel
Blaenau	upland
bod	dwelling
bryn	hill
bwlch	pass, col, gap or saddle
bychan	small
cae	field
caer	fort or encampment
capel	chapel
carreg	stone
castell	castle
cefn	back/ridge
clas	church
coch	red
coed	wood
craig	crag
croes	cross
cwm	valley
din	hillfort
dinas	large town or city

Welsh	English
du	black
dŵr	water
dyffryn	valley
eglwys	church
fach	small
fawr	large
ffordd	road
ffridd	pasture
ffynnon	spring or well
gallt	wooded slope
garn	cairn
garth	hill
glan	riverbank or shore
glas	green, blue, grey or silver
glyn	valley
gwaun	bog
gwyn	white
hafod	summer dwelling
heol	road
hewl	road
isaf	lower
llan	church
llyn	lake
maen	stone
mawr	big
melin	mill
moel	bare hill or mountain
morfa	seaside, marsh

Welsh	English
mynydd	mountain
nant	stream/valley
newydd	new
pant	valley
pen	end
penrhyn	headland
pentref	village/hamlet
pont	bridge
porth	port or harbour
pwll	pool
rhaeadr	waterfall
rhiw	hill
rhos	moor
rhyd	ford
sir	shire
stryd	street
traeth	shore or beach
uchaf	upper/highest

A simple guide to Welsh pronunciation
R is always pronounced and always rolled. Do not pronounce AR, ER, IR, OR, UR or YR as they are in English but just pronounce the short vowel with a rolling R after it, so ER will sounds a bit like the English 'air', IR, UR, YR as final syllables all sound like the English 'deer'; and YR as non-final syllables like the English 'fur'.

If there seem to be too many consonants at the end of a word (such as cefn) it is because vowels are sometimes omitted in Welsh. So cefn is pronounced k-ev-in).

Below is a simple guide to pronouncing consonants, vowels and the more common combinations found in Welsh place names.

Description	Example
Ae, Ai and Au as the 'y' in 'my'	e.g. mae (my), craig (crige)
Aw as the 'ow' in 'cow'	e.g. mawr (mour), fawr (vour)
C always hard as in 'cat'	e.g. cwm (coomb), Cymru (Kumree)
Ch soft as in the Scottish 'loch'	e.g. fach (vach)
Oe as the 'oy' in 'toy'	e.g. croes (croys)
Dd as the 'th' in 'the' or 'seethe'	e.g. bydd (beethe); carneddau (carneth-eye)
F as the 'v' in 'five'	e.g. afon (avon), fawr (vowr), fach (vach)
Ff as the 'f' in 'fight'	e.g. ffyrdd (firrth)
Ll is roughly the 'th' in theatre followed by 'l'	e.g. llan (thlan), llyn (thlin)
Ow as the 'ow' in 'cow'	e.g.Powys (Pow-iss)
Rh sounds as if the 'h' comes before the 'r'	e.g. rhyd (hrid)
U as the 'i' in 'pita'	e.g. Cymru (Kum-ree)
W as the 'oo' in 'zoo'	e.g. cwm (koom), bwlch (boolch)
Wy as the 'wi' in 'win'	e.g. wyddfa (with-va)
Yw as the 'ew' in 'yew'	e.g. byw (beeooh)

APPENDIX F
Further reading

Cardiff and the Marquesses of Bute, John Davies, (University of Wales Press, 2011)

Iconic Cycling Trails in Wales, Phil Horsley, (Gwasg Carreg Gwalch, 2017)

Owain Glyn Dŵr Prince of Wales, RR Davies (Y Lolfa, 2011)

The Celtic Trail, Rob Penn, (Pocket Mountains, 2008)

The Chapels of Wales, D Huw Owen, (Seren Books, 2012)

The Grand Designer: Third Marquess of Bute, Rosemary Hannah, (Birlinn, 2013)

The Story of Wales, Jon Gower, (BBC, 2013)

Wales Trails, Dave Lewis, (Self-published 2016 – see www.amazon.co.uk)

DOWNLOAD THE ROUTES
IN GPX FORMAT

All the routes in this guide are available for download from:

www.cicerone.co.uk/988/GPX

as GPX files. You should be able to load them into most formats of mobile device, whether GPS or smartphone.

When you go to this link, you will be asked for your email address and where you purchased the guide, and have the option to subscribe to the Cicerone e-newsletter.

www.cicerone.co.uk

LISTING OF CICERONE GUIDES

SCOTLAND

Backpacker's Britain:
  Northern Scotland
Ben Nevis and Glen Coe
Cycling in the Hebrides
Great Mountain Days in Scotland
Mountain Biking in Southern and
  Central Scotland
Mountain Biking in West and North
  West Scotland
Not the West Highland Way
Scotland
Scotland's Best Small Mountains
Scotland's Mountain Ridges
Scrambles in Lochaber
The Ayrshire and Arran Coastal Paths
The Border Country
The Borders Abbeys Way
The Cape Wrath Trail
The Great Glen Way
The Great Glen Way Map Booklet
The Hebridean Way
The Hebrides
The Isle of Mull
The Isle of Skye
The Skye Trail
The Southern Upland Way
The Speyside Way
The Speyside Way Map Booklet
The West Highland Way
Walking Highland Perthshire
Walking in Scotland's Far North
Walking in the Angus Glens
Walking in the Cairngorms
Walking in the Ochils, Campsie Fells
  and Lomond Hills
Walking in the Pentland Hills
Walking in the Southern Uplands
Walking in Torridon
Walking Loch Lomond and the
  Trossachs
Walking on Arran
Walking on Harris and Lewis
Walking on Rum and the Small Isles
Walking on the Orkney and Shetland
  Isles
Walking on Uist and Barra
Walking the Corbetts Vol 1 South of
  the Great Glen
Walking the Corbetts Vol 2 North of
  the Great Glen
Walking the Munros
  Vol 1 – Southern, Central and
  Western Highlands
Walking the Munros
  Vol 2 – Northern Highlands and
  the Cairngorms

West Highland Way Map Booklet
Winter Climbs Ben Nevis and
  Glen Coe
Winter Climbs in the Cairngorms

NORTHERN ENGLAND TRAILS

Hadrian's Wall Path
Hadrian's Wall Path Map Booklet
Pennine Way Map Booklet
The Coast to Coast Map Booklet
The Coast to Coast Walk
The Dales Way
The Dales Way Map Booklet
The Pennine Way

LAKE DISTRICT

Cycling in the Lake District
Great Mountain Days in the Lake
  District
Lake District Winter Climbs
Lake District: High Level and Fell
  Walks
Lake District: Low Level and Lake
  Walks
Mountain Biking in the Lake District
Outdoor Adventures with Children –
  Lake District
Scrambles in the Lake District –
  North
Scrambles in the Lake District –
  South
Short Walks in Lakeland
  Book 1: South Lakeland
Short Walks in Lakeland
  Book 2: North Lakeland
Short Walks in Lakeland
  Book 3: West Lakeland
The Cumbria Way
Tour of the Lake District
Trail and Fell Running in the Lake
  District

NORTH WEST ENGLAND
AND THE ISLE OF MAN

Cycling the Pennine Bridleway
Cycling the Way of the Roses
Isle of Man Coastal Path
The Lancashire Cycleway
The Lune Valley and Howgills
The Ribble Way
Walking in Cumbria's Eden Valley
Walking in Lancashire
Walking in the Forest of Bowland
  and Pendle
Walking on the Isle of Man
Walking on the West Pennine Moors
Walks in Ribble Country
Walks in Silverdale and Arnside

NORTH EAST ENGLAND,
YORKSHIRE DALES
AND PENNINES

Cycling in the Yorkshire Dales
Great Mountain Days in the
  Pennines
Mountain Biking in the Yorkshire
  Dales
South Pennine Walks
St Oswald's Way and
  St Cuthbert's Way
The Cleveland Way and the
  Yorkshire Wolds Way
The Cleveland Way Map Booklet
The North York Moors
The Reivers Way
The Teesdale Way
Trail and Fell Running in the
  Yorkshire Dales
Walking in County Durham
Walking in Northumberland
Walking in the North Pennines
Walking in the Yorkshire Dales:
  North and East
Walking in the Yorkshire Dales:
  South and West
Walks in Dales Country
Walks in the Yorkshire Dales

WALES AND WELSH BORDERS

Cycling Lôn Las Cymru
Glyndwr's Way
Great Mountain Days in Snowdonia
Hillwalking in Shropshire
Hillwalking in Wales – Vol 1
Hillwalking in Wales – Vol 2
Mountain Walking in Snowdonia
Offa's Dyke Map Booklet
Offa's Dyke Path
Ridges of Snowdonia
Scrambles in Snowdonia
The Ascent of Snowdon
The Ceredigion and Snowdonia
  Coast Paths
The Pembrokeshire Coast Path
Pembrokeshire Coast Path Map
  Booklet
The Severn Way
The Snowdonia Way
The Wales Coast Path
The Wye Valley Walk
Walking in Carmarthenshire
Walking in Pembrokeshire
Walking in the Forest of Dean
Walking in the South Wales Valleys
Walking in the Wye Valley
Walking on the Brecon Beacons
Walking on the Gower

For full information on all our guides,
books and eBooks, visit our website:
www.cicerone.co.uk

Walking – Trekking – Mountaineering – Climbing – Cycling

Over 40 years, Cicerone have built up an outstanding collection of over 300 guides, inspiring all sorts of amazing adventures.

Every guide comes from extensive exploration and research by our expert authors, all with a passion for their subjects. They are frequently praised, endorsed and used by clubs, instructors and outdoor organisations.

All our titles can now be bought as **e-books**, **ePubs** and **Kindle** files and we also have an online magazine – **Cicerone Extra** – with features to help cyclists, climbers, walkers and trekkers choose their next adventure, at home or abroad.

Our website shows any **new information** we've had in since a book was published. Please do let us know if you find anything has changed, so that we can publish the latest details. On our **website** you'll also find great ideas and lots of detailed information about what's inside every guide and you can buy **individual routes** from many of them online.

It's easy to keep in touch with what's going on at Cicerone by getting our monthly **free e-newsletter**, which is full of offers, competitions, up-to-date information and topical articles. You can subscribe on our home page and also follow us on **Facebook** and **Twitter** or dip into our **blog**.

Cicerone – the very best guides for exploring the world.

CICERONE

Juniper House, Murley Moss, Oxenholme Road, Kendal, Cumbria LA9 7RL
Tel: 015395 62069 info@cicerone.co.uk
www.cicerone.co.uk